Gin-spirational TOP PICKS

p15

Gin Lover's Guide To Europe

Hola! If you're heading away on a sunny continental break this year, our rundown of Euro gin hotspots is priceless!

p110

Half Baked

It turns out you CAN have your cake and eat it with this zesty yet sweet gin-infused triumph. Bake it, slice it, share it, devour it!

p128

Best Supporting Gins

From *The Great Gatsby* to *Casablanca*, gin has made its mark on the silver screen – check out our pick of the best gin flicks

Published in the UK by DC Thomson & Co Ltd © DC Thomson & Co Ltd 2024 Registered Office: DC Thomson & Co Ltd, Courier Buildings, 2 Albert Square, Dundee, Scotland, DD1 9QJ. If you would like to know how your data is handled by DC Thomson then please refer to our privacy policy www.dcthomson.co.uk/privacy-policies Distributed by Frontline Ltd, Stuart House, St John's St, Peterborough, Cambridgeshire, PE1 5DD. Tel: +44 (0) 1733 555161 www.frontlinedistribution.co.uk Export Distribution (excluding AU and NZ) by: Seymour Distribution Ltd, 2 East Poultry Avenue, London EC1A 9PT. Tel: +44 (0) 20 7429 4000 www.seymour.co.uk EU Representative Office: DC Thomson & Co Ltd c/o Findmypast Ireland, RBK House, Irishtown, Athlone, Co. Westmeath. N37 XP52. REPUBLIC OF IRELAND.

DC THOMSON

Shall We Be-Gin?

HELLO, welcome – and congratulations! You've made a very wise life decision and picked up a copy of the finest gin magazine around. *The Joy Of Gin* is the ultimate guide to living the good gin life. Within these merry pages, we shall take you, dear reader, on a whistle-stop voyage around the world in 80 incredible gins (with a quick detour to the moon) while we also detail the drink's scandalous history. Oo-er!

Discover the best distillery tours and greatest gin joints across the UK while our cocktail edit has a variety of fabulous gin-based creations to impress friends at your next house party. We even show you how to make your own gin at home as well as testing the best tonics, botanicals and garnishes to pair with your tipple.

And while we all love gin here, we do need to remind you to please drink responsibly – we won't be around to fetch you a bacon butty the morning after, so take it easy and savour every sip. Cheers!

Cover image: SHUTTERSTOCK

6

118

Contents

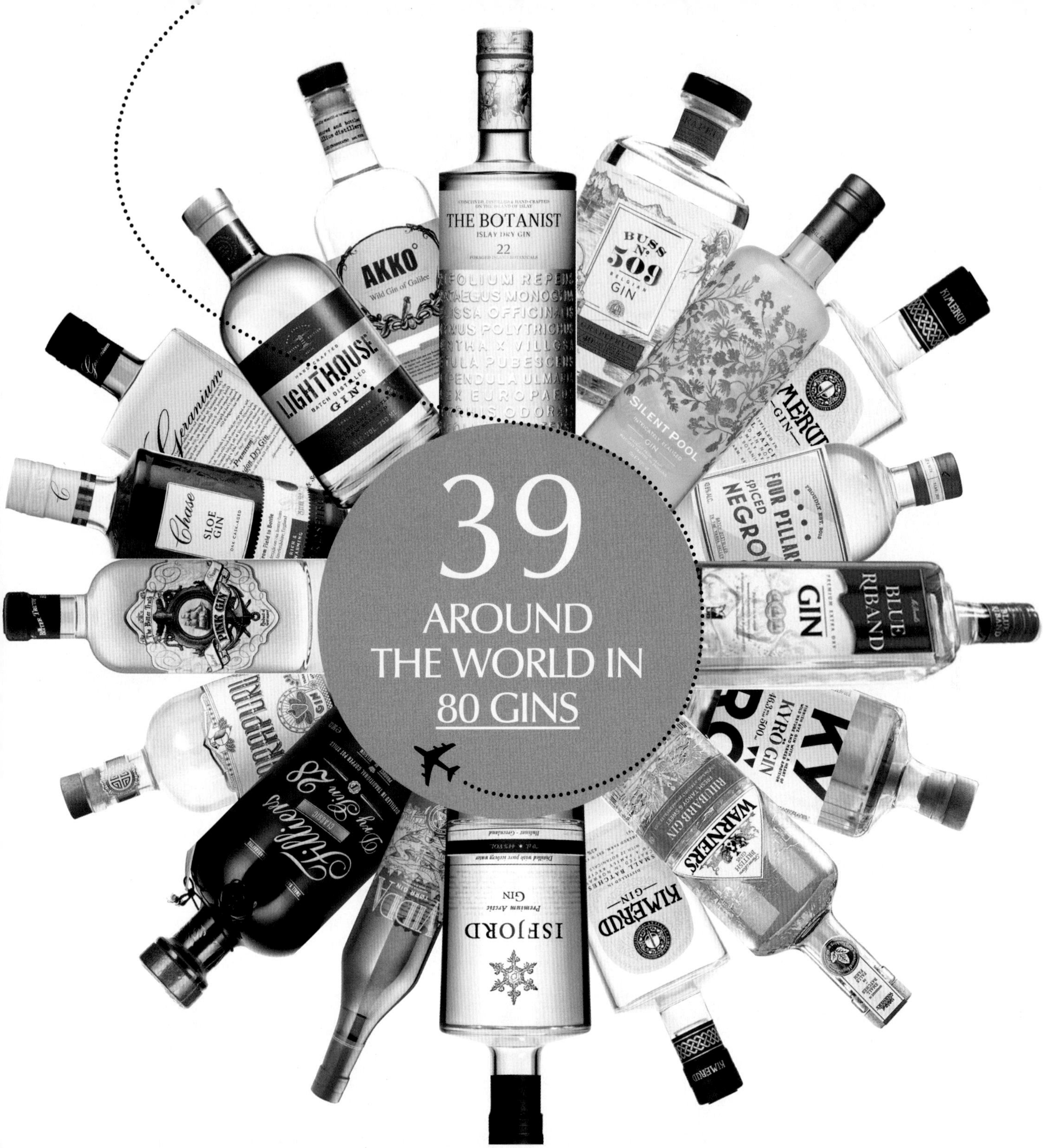
THE BOTANIST
ISLAY DRY GIN
AKKO
Wild Gin of Galilee
LIGHTHOUSE
BUSS N° 509
BELGIAN
GIN
SILENT POOL
GIN
KIMERUD
GIN
FOUR PILLARS
SPICED
NEGRONI
BLUE
RIBAND
GIN
KYRÖ GIN
WARNER'S
RHUBARB GIN
ISFJORD
Premium Arctic
GIN
Chase
SLOE
GIN
Geranium
PINK GIN
Hillier's
Dry Gin 28
39
AROUND
THE WORLD IN
80 GINS

80
DABACHRO

68
BAR

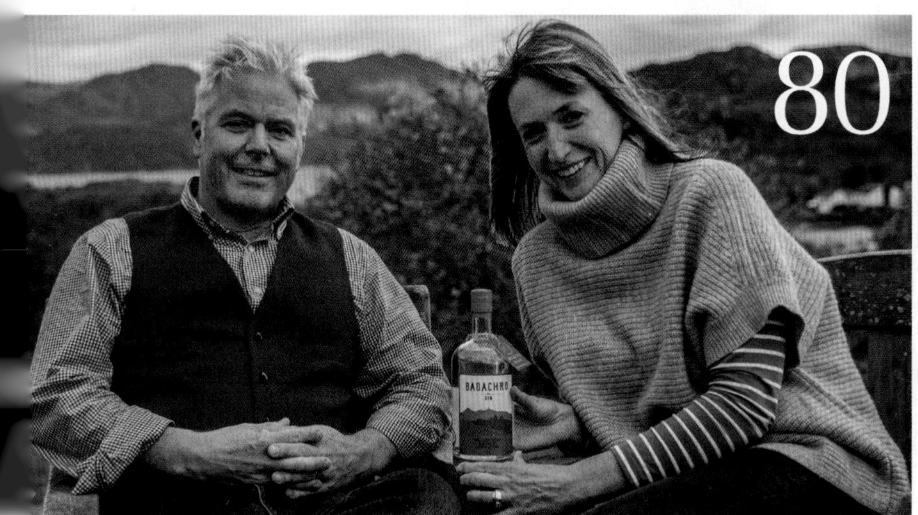

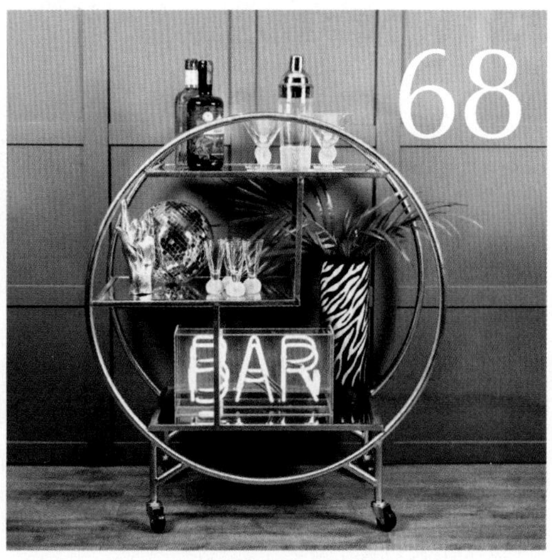

TOURED And Tested

We travelled the UK, trying out the top gin distillery tours to find out which ones offer the best value for money

FROM £30

Eden Mill / Edinburgh

Eden Mill are currently in the midst of a full redevelopment of their St Andrews distillery but that doesn't mean you have to miss out on their unique tasting tour. The brewery's Edinburgh Experience brings the spirit of St Andrews to the Scottish capital and offers an insight into their fruity and floral Love Gin while you enjoy three cocktails – one of which you'll make yourself!

FROM £100

Greensand Ridge / Kent

This won't be the cheapest tour on your gin journey, but it'll easily be one of the best. Set in the enchanting Kent countryside, Greensand Ridge's Victorian coach house-turned-distillery creates the perfect atmosphere of premium intimacy, where you can sip on a seasonal cocktail and soak up gin history, before getting botanical savvy and distilling a bottle of your own handmade gin.

FROM £25

City Of London / London

You're guaranteed a warm welcome and brilliant day out at the City Of London's fab guided tour. Discover the history of gin in the capital before learning about the distiller's own gin making techniques. The tour includes a G&T on arrival followed by a four-flight gin tasting so you are well catered for! You can even head to their stylish bar afterwards for a post-tour treat or two.

FROM £25

Sipsmith / London

Sipsmith really is a must-visit for gin lovers. It's more than just a tour; it's a spectacle. You can opt for either the tour and the tasting, or upgrade to The Ultimate Gin Cocktail Masterclass, where you can learn the techniques endorsed by Sipsmith's world-renowned Master Distiller Jared Brown and learn the top tips for shaking, stirring and throwing cocktails for full effect.

FROM £25

Silent Pool / Albury

It's samples galore at the Silent Pool Distillery. Their range of gins and cordials – and vodka if you're that way inclined – is a truly delicious experience, made all the more appealing by the low entry cost. Not only will you get change from £30, but you'll be treated to a fascinating history. You'll even get a fiver off at the shop too. Bargain!

Just The TONIC

Try Aqua Monaco Organic Herbal Tonic for a more complex tonic hit.

10/10

Aqua Monaco Tonic

aquamonaco.com

Using mineral water from deep beneath the glacial plains around Munich, Aqua Monaco drinks are pure and smooth. This particular tonic blends tangy quinine, natural lemon extracts and other aromatics to make it the ideal mixer for long drinks. Our testers also enjoyed this one on its own with ice and lemon – perfect on a hot day!
Mix with: Tarquin's Dry Gin, once voted the best gin in the world!

7/10

Schweppes Lavender & Orange Blossom Tonic

schweppes.eu

Schweppes Classic Tonic Water is the oldest soft drink in the world, but they're far from being stuck in the past. This lavender and orange blossom tonic is deliciously flowery and fruity. It tastes best paired with a dry or floral gin – or just on its own! If you like this, you might want to give their hibiscus tonic a try too.
Mix with: A dry drink like Sipsmith London Dry Gin or something floral like Caorunn.

Add a sprig of rosemary to your G & floral T.

Grapefruit, lavender, cranberry, artisan organic unicorn tears harvested by mermaids… picking a tonic has become almost as tricky as selecting your bottle of gin. Which water will enhance your gin's unique taste? And which are delicious on their own? We put them to the test!

Words: ALEXANDRIA TURNER

8/10

Jack Rudy Cocktail Co. Classic Tonic Syrup

jackrudycocktailco.com

Jack Rudy was a modern Southern American gentleman who had a penchant for engineering, craftsmanship, drinking and his wife's cooking, and is the inspiration behind this, his great-grandchildren's business. Formerly known as the Jack Rudy Small Batch Tonic, this is a classic quinine concentrate, mixed with botanicals and sweetened with real cane sugar. Our testers had never tried a tonic syrup before, but they were pleasantly surprised by how versatile it is, adding a hit of elegance to any drink. A little goes a long way.
Mix with: Classic clear spirits like Tanqueray No. 10 or Stolichnaya. Dim the lights and stick on some jazz to get that real American speakeasy feel!

30 Servings in each bottle!

7/10

Ledger's Tonic Water & Cinnamon

ledgerstonic.com

The history of Ledger's is a fascinating one. The brand's namesake, Charles Ledger, was an alpaca farmer who discovered the ledgeriana cinchona, the plant which is the source of quinine, in 1864. He pioneered the development of tonic and soda and introduced stevia as a natural sweetener instead of sugar or artificial syrups. Their tonics are available in many flavours like liquorice and tangerine, but cinnamon was a firm favourite with our testers who claim that it "tastes like Christmas".

Mix with: Either a smooth tipple like Brockmans Gin, or for the ultimate Christmas hit, Edinburgh Gin Spiced Orange Liqueur.

9/10

Double Dutch Cranberry & Ginger Tonic Water

doubledutchdrinks.com

Founded by Dutch twin sisters Joyce and Raissa de Haas out of their frustration at a lack of tasty tonics to mix with their gin, Double Dutch tonics are a delight. Balancing the astringency of quinine with sweet and sour cranberry, this tonic is dry and refreshing at the same time. The de Haas twins call it "the essence of seduction" and who are we to disagree?

Mix with: Try a darker gin like Bathtub Cask Aged Gin, Dictador Premium Colombian Aged Gin or Filliers Barrel Aged Gin.

The Double Dutch Skinny Tonic also got high praise from our testers.

6/10

Gents Swiss Roots Tonic Water

gents.ch

Already popular across Switzerland, Denmark and Germany, this Swiss tonic has finally made its way to UK shores. It's the go-to tonic water for mixologists across Europe due to its neutral-bitter quinine and bitter liquorice notes. The tonic combines lemon with raw materials from the Lake Zurich region, which is famous for its glaciers that run down from the Glarus Alps, a UNESCO world heritage site.

Mix with: Delicious gins from the continent: nginious! Swiss Blended Gin, Kongsgaard Raw Gin from Denmark and Monkey 47 which is made in the Black Forest.

7/10

Macario Tonica

macariocompany.it

In 1950s Italy, Nonna Vittoria Macario would spend her summer preparing refreshing drinks for loved ones. Her family began a small homemade production and it prospered for some years; then the founder, becoming elderly, decided to close the business. Fast-forward to the 21st century, and one of her grandsons has resurrected her drinks! This is an excellent Italian tonic that is full of delicate, fine bubbles, and a great choice for drinkers who don't like the bitterness of quinine. This tonic is much more citrusy, sweet and herby than typical offerings.

Mix with: Something high in flavour like Martin Miller's Gin, Bloom Gin and Slingsby Gin.

The Best GIN DENS In London

Words: SIAN MEADES

Every bar and pub in London will pour you a G&T, but there are some establishments that go all out to knock your juniper-loving socks off

Mr Fogg's Gin Club

From the outside, Mr Fogg's Gin Club looks like little more than a busy pub. It's an odd location – around the back of Oxford Circus just on the fringes of not-quite Soho – but this bar, housed in what was once The London Gin Club, is a fine choice for any gin fan. Step back in time with its Olde Worlde interiors and try on a truly dazzling collection of vintage hats on while you drink and socialise – it's a lot of fun. The bar snacks will ruin your dinner, too.

22 Great Chapel St, W1F 8FR

Dukes

If you're of the martini drinking persuasion, there's one hotel bar that is the undisputed king: Dukes. A martini here is a legendary experience – frequently visited by James Bond author Ian Fleming, the bar is said to be the inspiration for the classic line "shaken, not stirred". The intimate yet timeless surrounds provide warmth while the world-class bartender team will ensure you have an unforgettable Mayfair gin adventure.

35 St James's Place, SW1A 1NY

The Gin Bar At Holborn

If you're indecisive about your tipple, head to The Rosewood in Holborn to sample a little something from the largest gin collection in London. The Gin Bar at Holborn Dining Rooms houses over 500 gins and 30 different tonics. That equates to 14,000 combinations of gin and tonic (we were too tipsy to do the maths, but we'll take their word for it). Don't try and drink them all in one evening.

252 High Holborn, WC1V 7EN

Martello Hall

It's not just the dozens of spirits that Martello Hall stock that make this upstart Hackney bar and micro-distillery worth seeking out during a visit to the capital. Maybe you'll want to try their gin blending or cocktail masterclasses or sip a trendy G&T while you wait for them to serve you pizza from their own wood oven. And if you stay on late, be sure to enjoy a boogie with friends. This definitely isn't your average central London bar.

137 Mare St, E8 3RH

Two One Four

This little gin joint is hidden under a restaurant and it's well worth scouting out, especially during happy hour. Whatever your gin of choice (and there are over 100 on offer), pair it with the Bermondsey Tonic Water, a subtly flavoured companion with a bright, bubbly zing – it's handmade in London. Oh, and while you're in the area head to Jensen's Distillery, for a mug of their hot gin.

214 Bermondsey St, SE1 3TQ

Sub Club

Our rundown of the UK's best gin subscription boxes...

Words: ALEXANDRIA TURNER

I Love Gin

ilovegin.com

If you're looking for a budget way to enjoy gin, then look no further than I Love Gin's monthly subscription. Every month they'll send you two miniature gins and two tonics for you to mix at home – that's enough to make four delicious G&Ts, plus you'll get a recipe booklet with the perfect serves and garnishes, and info on the featured drinks. You'll also get exclusive member-only discounts in their online shop, plus access to other great deals.

Price: £17.50 with free delivery.
Payment options: Monthly, 3/6/12 months, plus one-off gift boxes.
What do you get? A brand new G&T tasting box each month.

Little Gin Box

littleginbox.com

The neat bottles inside each Little Gin Box pack a punch. The selection is spot-on, featuring craft gins from all over the UK. This is a particularly great choice if you want a cheap treat for yourself, or you're gifting it to a friend or family member.

Price: £11 with free delivery.
Payment options: 1, 2, 3, 5, 6, 10 or 12 months, all for a one-off charge. Or there is the monthly rolling membership which you can cancel at any time.
What do you get? Two 50ml bottles of carefully selected gin, tasting notes and distiller's view.

Craft Gin Club

craftginclub.co.uk

With thousands of members, this is the number one gin subscription club in the UK – and it's easy to see why. Receiving a full-size bottle of gin every month – or to a selection of frequencies of your choosing – this is perfect for gin lovers who wish to share a drink with friends. The snacks and treats enhance the package, giving you all the ingredients you need for a fabulous, and possibly pretty tipsy, night in.

Price: £45 with free delivery.
Payment options: Monthly, bi-monthly and quarterly.
What do you get? A full-size bottle of gin, a selection of perfectly paired tonics, mixers, foodie treats and a glossy magazine.

Think Gin Club

thinkginclub.com

Boasting the best gin brands in the UK and beyond, subscribers receive a different, full-size bottle of gin every month. As well as your monthly gin fix, you'll get tasting notes, cocktail recipes and complimentary gifts. It really is great value and there's no big contract with this one – you can cancel any time or pause your membership indefinitely, making it perfect for commitment-phobes.

Price: £44 with free delivery. **Payment options:** Monthly, bi-monthly and quarterly.
What do you get? A full-size bottle of gin, complimentary mixers, snacks, tasting notes and cocktail recipes. New subscribers receive a free giant gin glass, plus 10% off their first box.

Words: LESLEY MANUEL

The Gin Lover's Garden

Ooh, we've come over all green-fingered! Stuff a window box full of gin-loving herbs...

- Rosemary is a great gin twin and is scientifically proven to restore memory. Now you'll remember every gincident from the night before…
- Mint brings freshness to your gin cocktails with the added bonus of settling an upset stomach. Did someone say hair of the dog?
- Lavender will populate your home with gorgeous scent, fill you with calm and top off floral gins to perfection.
- Freeze dill with blueberries in ice cubes to make the best accompaniment for clean, Scandinavian gins.
- Basil is especially good paired with strawberry or cucumber.
- Or pack in your greens with a Basil Smash – put 25ml of lemon juice into a cocktail shaker with a handful of basil leaves and gently muddle together. Top up with gin, 15ml of sugar syrup and ice. Shake and strain.

NEVER Underdressed

Accessorise your G&T, darling, with these quirky tips for a top tipple

Top Twists

Which citrus will best complement your gin refreshments? We conducted a (not at all scientific) survey which revealed red grapefruit as the bartender's choice, followed by orange. Yuzu is also big this summer in tonics and twists.

It's Five O'Clock Somewhere

Any time is cocktail time with The Bitter Truth Cocktail Bitters Traveler's Set. The mysterious little tin contains five bitters to add a touch of magic to your gin tipple. Try the included recipes and match a cocktail to your location – we're all over a Dry Martini as we watch a Mediterranean sunset. Best of all, it's cabin bag friendly, so ditch the toiletries and pack this instead. the-bitter-truth.com

The Gin CURIOSITY CABINET

An odd bunch, we gin drinkers...

Words: LORI PETRIE

WITH its rich and varied history, gin – or rather the enthusiasts who drink it – have undoubtedly been involved in some rather unusual affairs…

Breaking The Ice

Two centuries ago, hundreds of merry Londoners stood precariously on the frozen surface of the Thames, enjoying the sights and sounds of an impromptu frosty festival. Revellers warmed themselves up by sipping on hot gin, complemented by plenty of festive gingerbread. We might not see another Frost Fair again, but at least we can still party like it's 1814!

Hair Of The Dog

The decadence and excess of the Roaring '20s required an especially effective hangover cure. The remedy of choice for suffering flapper girls of New York? Gin mixed with tomato juice. Easy enough to settle your stomach with all the hydrating benefits and vitamins you need to balance yourself out, plus an extra juniper kick. Bloody Mary who?

GIN

BATCH | ALC./VOL

YEAR | mL

PRIVATE COLLECTION

Sweet Treats

The Ramos Gin Fizz might just be one of the greatest cocktails known to man. It's basically a dessert in a glass with the added bonus of gin. An enterprising cocktail master by the name of Eben Freeman has found a way to turn this fluffy delight into a beautifully compact marshmallow. Delicious, portable and a lot less work to clean up. What more could you want?

Please Breathe Responsibly

A pop-up bar in London gives you the chance to inhale your standard gin and tonic as a vapour. We feel that removing the actual drinking aspect of, well, drinking takes much of the joy out of imbibing our favourite gins. What's the use in having all of these interesting new flavour combinations if we can't taste them? Is aerosolised booze the future of pubs? We certainly hope not.

The Gin Lover's Guide To EUROPE

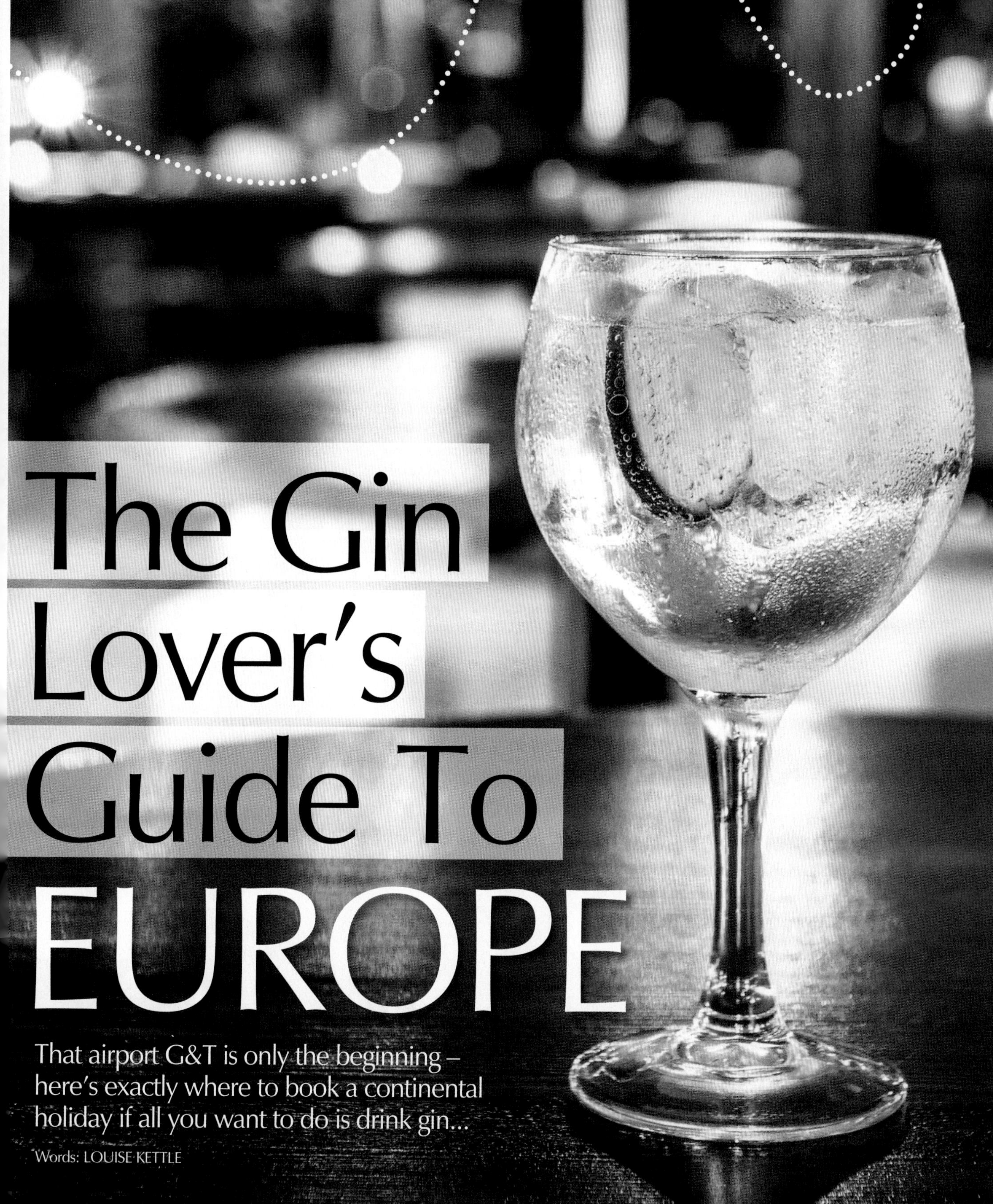

That airport G&T is only the beginning – here's exactly where to book a continental holiday if all you want to do is drink gin...

Words: LOUISE KETTLE

BARCELONA

SPAIN

SPAIN loves gin. It's become one of the world's largest consumers of the stuff — which may or may not be down to their delightfully hefty measures. Expect a 50:50 ratio in your gintonic (yes, ditch the ampersand). The humble lemon slice your auntie still slops into her slimline won't cut the mustard here either – flavoured tonics and carefully considered fruits and herbs are tailored to each blend.

Spaniards treat gintonic as a "copa" – an after-dinner drink to be enjoyed long into the night. We think it works perfectly as a tapas companion too, acting as a refreshing interlude between mouthfuls of salty chorizo and manchego.

STAY

Casa Gràcia

casagraciabcn.com

Nestled between several popular gin bars, this friendly hostel makes the ideal base to explore the city. There are private rooms as well as dorms, with prices to suit most budgets.

DRINK

The Original Old Fashioned

theoriginaloldfashioned.com

Modelled on a speakeasy, it'd be criminal not to pay this place a visit. We loved the relaxed atmosphere and knowledgeable bar staff who are happy to go off-menu and create something to suit your mood.

EAT

El Nacional

elnacionalbcn.com/el-restaurante

The perfect place for the indecisive foodie. Four restaurants and four bars provide plenty of options, covering meat, fish, tapas and rice – after which you can indulge in a copa or two at the reasonably-priced cocktail bar.

SWEDEN

VEN

THE island of Ven is located between Denmark and Sweden and can be reached by ferry from Copenhagen (ventrafiken.se). Despite its small size (4.5km by 2.4km, to be exact), this little gem has its very own distillery, Spirit of Hven, which produces their Organic Gin and Organic Navy Strength Gin.

STAY

Backafallsbyn Hotel
backafallsbyn.se

Why stay anywhere else when you can stay at the distillery? The on-site hotel has 36 small cottages, and offers various packages which include distillery tours, spa treatments and meals from the excellent restaurant.

DRINK

The Whisky Bar
backafallsbyn.se

Staggering distance from your bed is the hotel bar, but don't let the name put you off. It holds a great selection of beers and ales as well as the in-house gin.

EAT

Restaurang Ella
restaurangella.se

Named after the owner's mother, this bijou restaurant by the sea serves delicious local produce in a stunning setting. A must-visit.

GOTHENBURG'S BEST BARS

Sweden's second-largest city is known for its night life, and its compact size means it's easy to barhop by foot. Skål!

Steampunk Bar
atsteampunkbar.se

We insist you check out the 70-strong gin and tonic menu immediately (see website), which left us delirious with indecision. Some are even served with dry ice.

Dorsia
dorsia.se

This luxe boutique hotel is made for romantics. The Salon is the perfect place to unwind with a Swedish gin, or head up to the roof terrace. Not advised for minimalists.

Stranger
strangergbg.com

We booked our flights based on the strength of this cocktail alone: The Slushie – gin, Campari, Aperol, sweet vermouth, grapefruit and watermelon.

BERLIN

GERMANY

MONKEY 47 is only the beginning when it comes to German gin; the number of distillers is now said to run into the hundreds. It seems the capital is still the best place to go on a posh bar crawl, with Berliners' love for G&T rivalling that of Barcelonians.

STAY

Hotel Palace

palace.de

Central location, pool, gym, spa, various dining options – this chic hotel ticks most travellers' boxes. You might not even bother leaving it, considering the bar's called House of Gin. With 150 varieties to choose from and a tasting menu to get stuck in to, we recommend a long stay.

DRINK

Windhorst

windhorst-bar.de

The Windhorst is a hidden little haven nestled in Berlin's bustling heart. This chilled-out gem offers sophisticated ambiance paired with impeccable service. Trust us when we say that after just one drink, you'll want to stay all night.

EAT

Dicke Wirtin

dicke-wirtin.de

Line your stomach with some proper German grub at this charming bar-restaurant. You'll need to make a reservation due to its popularity with locals and tourists alike – expect a crowded, buzzy atmosphere. Don't leave without trying the pork schnitzel…

AMSTERDAM

THE NETHERLANDS

GIN'S Dutch relative jenever, from which gin evolved, is reason enough to visit the Netherlands. But like the other European cities on our hotlist, gin and tonic fever has hit Amsterdam too, meaning you can happily indulge in both. Sip canal-side while people watching, or explore the many specialist gin and jenever bars.

DRINK

Proeflokaal A. Van Wees
proeflokaalvanwees.nl

A characterful bar serving a great selection of jenever – we recommend having a tasting session of several. Simple, delicious food is also on offer should all that quaffing work up an appetite.

EAT

Pompadour
pompadour.amsterdam

Set in the delightful Nine Streets area, this pretty patisserie makes an ideal stop-off during a saunter round the array of shops and boutiques. Don't forget to Instagram your cake before you eat it.

STAY

Hotel Estherea
estherea.nl

This hotel completely charmed us – the decadent interiors, the lovely staff, the free cake and coffee, the cat...! Its location is within walking distance to most of the main attractions yet away from the bustle of Dam Square's stag and hen contingent. The bar is top-notch too, serving cocktails and snacks until late.

How To Drink Jenever

- Serve chilled and neat in a small tulip glass.
- Knock one back before a beer for a "Kopstoot" (a blow to your head).
- Jonge jenever can be treated like vodka and mixed with cola, tonic, soda and lemon, or used in cocktails.

Pictures: SHUTTERSTOCK

England's FINEST GIN BARS

Words: SIAN MEADES

Whether you have a penchant for Plymouth or London Gin is your thing, this green and pleasant land has some really great drinking holes...

WC Gin Closet, Newcastle

Tiny but perfectly formed, the WC Gin Closet in fact claims to be the UK's smallest gin bar but don't let the intimate interior fool you – it still offers an extensive selection of over 70 gins. The perfect place to cosy up with a loved one!

4a High Bridge, NE1 6BX

The Old Bell Inn, Saddleworth

So large is the collection of gin at The Old Bell Inn, this emporium just on the edge of the Peak District once made its way into the *Guinness Book Of World Records*. They house a staggering 1,100 gins – just don't try to get through them all in the one night!

Huddersfield Road, OL3 5EG

Atlas, Manchester

Gin is very much the thing in Atlas in Deansgate – hundreds of them feature in the bar's "Gin Bible". The team here love gin so much that they even host a gin masterclass so you can learn about your tipple as you drink it.

376 Deansgate, M3 4LY

The Distillery Gin Bar, Bath

Bath's cocktail bar scene is small but vibrant. The Distillery Gin Bar is undoubtedly the finest place in the city for gin lovers and it's home to infamous Bath Gin. The cocktail bar serves modern cocktails inspired by global travels

3 Queen St, BA1 1HE

The Florist, Liverpool

Be sure to bring your camera-phone for what is surely the prettiest gin bar in the country. Immerse yourself in the sensory delights of cherry blossom trees and floral walls, carefully crafted floral cocktails and culinary delights. Sheer heaven.

24 Hardman St, L1 9AX

Mother's Ruin: THE SCANDALOUS HISTORY OF GIN

Everything you wanted to know about our favourite tipple – and a few things you didn't!

Words: WILL BATTLE Illustrations: BALAZS LORINCZI

?

“AWFUL LOT OF EFFORT JUST TO GET DRUNK IF YOU ASK ME!”

1500 BC

The first people to get crazy with juniper berries were the ancient Egyptians. They had their own plants, but started to import other juniper varieties from Greece. Tutankhamun was buried with multiple varieties of the berry and ancient recipes found on papyrus used juniper in a cure for tapeworms. Good to know.

765 BC

Step aside steroids! The performance-enhancing drug of choice for the original ancient Greek Olympians was the juniper berry. The Greeks believed that they gave athletes increased stamina – and there's no drug testing for juniper! If only gin was that good for you.

1055 AD

When the Moors came to Italy in the Middle Ages, they brought with them knowledge of distillation. Benedictine Monks used this knowledge to start making alcohol. They would brew up pretty much anything, including the juniper from the nearby hills.

1495 AD

In the Netherlands, a recipe was written for a spirit distilled from wine which included nutmeg, cinnamon, galanga, seeds of paradise, cloves, ginger, sage, cardamom and juniper. Distilled juniper mixed with botanicals? That's the world's first gin recipe!

1575 AD

The Bols family set up a distillery in Amsterdam and began producing juniper flavoured spirits and liqueurs. Based on Professor Sylvius de Bouve's medicine recipe, jenever became the first ever brand of gin in world.

"THIS GIN CONTAINS TURPENTINE AND SULPHURIC ACID, WHO WANTS SOME?"

1582 AD

Distillers realised that it's much easier to produce large amounts of alcohol by fermenting and distilling grain instead of wine. As the Thirty Years War took hold, French grape supplies were interrupted and demand for Dutch grain spirit increased.

1648 AD

English soldiers returning from the Thirty Years War brought back a taste for Dutch jenever and stories of how drinking it had made the Dutch soldiers so much braver. This is where we get the idea of "Dutch courage" from.

1723 AD

A Dutch king and cheap distilling led to gin becoming the drink of choice in England. London was struck by a gin craze of the worst kind. Mothers would neglect their children and even sell them, just to get even the poorest-quality gin. Mother's ruin indeed!

1757 AD

After eight different acts of Parliament to limit the sales of gin, a poor harvest caused grain distilling to be banned in the UK completely. They feared people would make booze instead of bread! Don't worry, distilling was brought back three years later.

1828 AD

The first pubs began partnering with brewers to become desirable venues. Henry B. Fearon worked with gin distillers and opened the world's first gin palace. This desire for opulence spread and by the late 1940s there were over 5,000 gin palaces in London alone!

1831 AD

Aeneas Coffey perfected a new method of distilling gin that got rid of the idea of batches, producing gin without stopping. This method led to the creation of London Dry Gin and formed the basis of how all modern gin is produced. Thanks, Aeneas!

1870 AD

People had been mixing quinine with drinks to deal with malaria since Roman times, but in 1870 Schweppes started selling the first ever fizzy quinine tonic, calling it Indian Tonic Water. British colonists in India loved their gin, so the G&T was born!

1920 AD

Prohibition hit the US, which made drinking gin a little trickier. Bathtub gin was invented: it was dangerous, but good enough to give us the term "to die for"! Americans also tried to smuggle in British gins through Canada and the West Indies. Some people will do anything for a martini!

1956 AD

By the mid 1950s, soda guns, cocktail premix and ice machines had made making cocktails easier than ever. Sadly, this meant quick and easy drinks like vodka were in and taking time to make a proper gin cocktail was out.

1988 AD

When gin sales were at their lowest, a bright blue bottle brought eyes back on the booze. Bombay Sapphire launched, then many other major gins lowered their alcohol content to compete. Gin was back, then a resurgence of small producers made it cool again.

"GIN MAKING'S REALLY GOING DOWN THE TUBES!"

NEW YORK'S Greatest Gin Joints

Words: RACHAEL KILGOUR

Beat the schlep – we've pinpointed exactly where you need to be in the Big Apple

Dear Irving

The real selling point of this is its fabulous rooftop bar. Sipping a top-shelf gin while gazing over a gorgeous view of the Hudson River? Oh, yes please! They also offer cocktail classes where you can learn history and technique from one of their expert cocktail educators.

310 West 40th Street

The Lovelace

You'll find this gem in New York's Financial District, and won't regret hunting it down. There's a beautiful main bar with an impressive cocktail menu, some nice outdoor seating and even a beer room in the back for your non-gin-loving friends.

66 Pearl St

Bathtub Gin

You can't visit New York without hitting up a hidden bar, right? Half the fun is finding this place, tucked behind an unassuming coffee shop and catapulting you back to the Prohibition Era. With pages of gin cocktails, burlesque dancers and jazz singers – you can leave your cares at the door.

132 9th Avenue, Manhattan

Weather Up

This slick, Prohibition-style watering hole in the hip neighbourhood of Tribeca will wow you with its craft cocktails and sophisticated bar snacks. Be sure to order a Poet's Dream which is their version of a gin martini – thoroughly delish!

159 Duane St

The Winslow

With a strong gin focus and British nibbles on the menu, this is your home away from home. Their monthly gin clubs host a different gin distiller each time, and offer a welcome cocktail and promise lively conversation with other guests and the distillers themselves.

243 East 14th Street

The flavour of your gin is all down to the power of plants. Surely this means we can include our favourites as part of our five a day?

Oh, That TASTES

Words: LESLEY MANUEL

The Core Four

By law, gin must contain juniper, so the taste of juniper is the taste of gin. It has bittersweet notes of woody pine resin and green citrus.

Coriander seed is a brilliant blending partner, pairing with the juniper to boost the peppery notes and add hints of sage, citrus and a little bit of Miss Havisham mustiness.

Angelica is very similar to juniper, bringing dry woody, earthy and musky notes to the gin party. It amplifies and helps to marry all the flavours together.

Made from the dried root of an iris, orris binds the flavour notes and stops more delicate scents from disappearing. It adds a floral perfume to the blend.

You'll often find the following added too...

- Liquorice root to soften and sweeten
- Orange and lemon peel for fresh, crisp, citrus flavours
- Grains of Paradise to deepen the woody, peppery flavours

If you're a fan of a crisp, dry G&T, choose Tanqueray. This perfectly balanced gin has four distinct ingredients for an unrivalled flavour. It has been voted the Bartender's Favourite Gin in the past! diageo.com

If you're designated driver – or fancy a relaxing G&T without the morning-after fuzz – there are now plenty of alcohol-free gins on the market to choose from. Our favourite is the Sipsmith FreeGlider, crafted with juniper and citrus, and ideal for those moments of moderation. sipsmith.com

Fire It Up!

Choose a gin featuring any of these botanical pairings to turn up the heat...

- Cardamom – aromatic warmth
- Sweet and woody cinnamon
- Cubeb berries for spicy and peppery pine notes
- Ginger root for powerful, dry, hot spice
- Chilli for a hot kick
- Warming, sweet nutmeg
- Star anise for a liquorice twist

NICE!

Pictures: SHUTTERSTOCK

Sweet & Sour

You're spoiled for choice if fresh citrus or sweet florals are your thing. Delicious pairings to look out for in a gin are...

- Apple
- Cucumber
- Grapefruit
- Pomegranate
- Summer berries
- Rhubarb
- Lavender
- Rose
- Hibiscus
- Geranium
- Elderflower

You'll often find us of a Friday indulging in a Hendrick's. With a curious infusion of both rose and cucumber, top up with tonic and strawberry slices for summer in a glass! hendricksgin.com

THE RECIPE

Make your own gin!

Words: LESLEY MANUEL Illustrations: KIRK HOUSTON

No, we're not suggesting you set up a dodgy still in the shed*, but steeping botanicals to make compound gin is easy – and completely legal. Hurrah!

*Not at all legal!

1 litre jar
Sterilise with boiling water
+ 70cl vodka

Add botanicals –
40g juniper berries
10g coriander seeds
½ cinnamon stick
½ liquorice root
2 cardamom pods

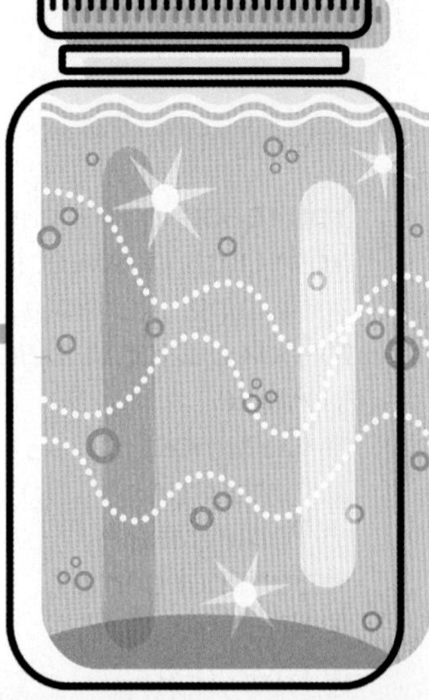

Develop in the jar for 2 days
Filter again
Oh look – a lovely amber gin!

Tonic
GARNISH

Gin o'clock!

Let's Talk About…(ssshh – whisper it now) Vodka!

Ideally use a good quality vodka for this project. If you wouldn't drink it, don't make gin with it.

However, if all you have is a random bottle you once stole from a party, a water filter jug is your new best friend. Passing the vodka through the filter two or three times before starting will take the fire out of your hooch for a softer gin.

You can filter again at the end of the process to make a lighter colour gin.

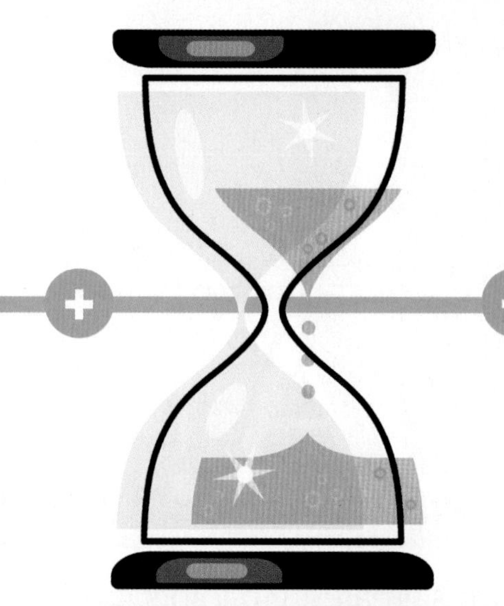

Infuse for 24 hours in a cool dark place
Have a taste – juniper flavour should be developing

+ 1 piece each of orange and lemon peel
Bitter pith removed

Taste again
If you like it, sieve out the botanicals
Strain through a coffee filter

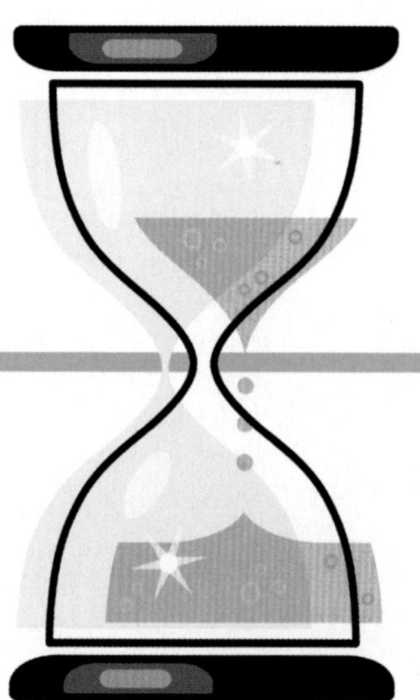

24 hours
Shake once
Don't over infuse

IECHYD DA!

Words: MAGGIE SWINBURNE

That's Welsh for cheers, fact fans! Here are some of Cymru's greatest gin joints...

The Bull's Head Inn, Beaumaris

Ideally located on the picturesque coast of Anglesey, Beaumaris's stunning Victorian pier is perfect for an early morning stroll to watch the sailing boats go by after a night in the bar at The Bull spent sampling their ever-growing selection of gins, ranging from dry to fruity to floral.

Castle Street, LL58 8AP

Potted Pig, Cardiff

Trot along and you'll be squealing with delight and wriggling your curly tail when you see what's on offer in this delicious little restaurant, set in an old bank vault. They have a wonderful selection of gins with dozens of different brands on offer.

27 High Street, CF10 1PU

The Fat Boar, Wrexham

A newcomer in Wrexham's city centre, The Fat Boar has quickly garnered an enviable reputation for its wholesome pub grub. Oh – and the small matter of its huge gin offering to go with it! Be sure to stick your snout in.

11 Yorke St, LL13 8LW

Lab 22, Cardiff

Look for the logo lighting up the corner of Mill Lane… as something weird and wonderful is being created. Follow the mysterious sounds and delicious scents to find Lab 22, one of the most prestigious and unusual cocktail bars in the world, never mind Wales.

22 Caroline Street, CF10 1FG

Gin & Juice, Swansea

Oh, we do like to be beside the seaside, don't we? Well, this popular rooftop bar and restaurant overlooks the beautiful Mumbles seafront and it's well worth a visit. Soak in the coastline while sampling some of the 350 gins on offer.

Oyster Wharf, SA3 4DN

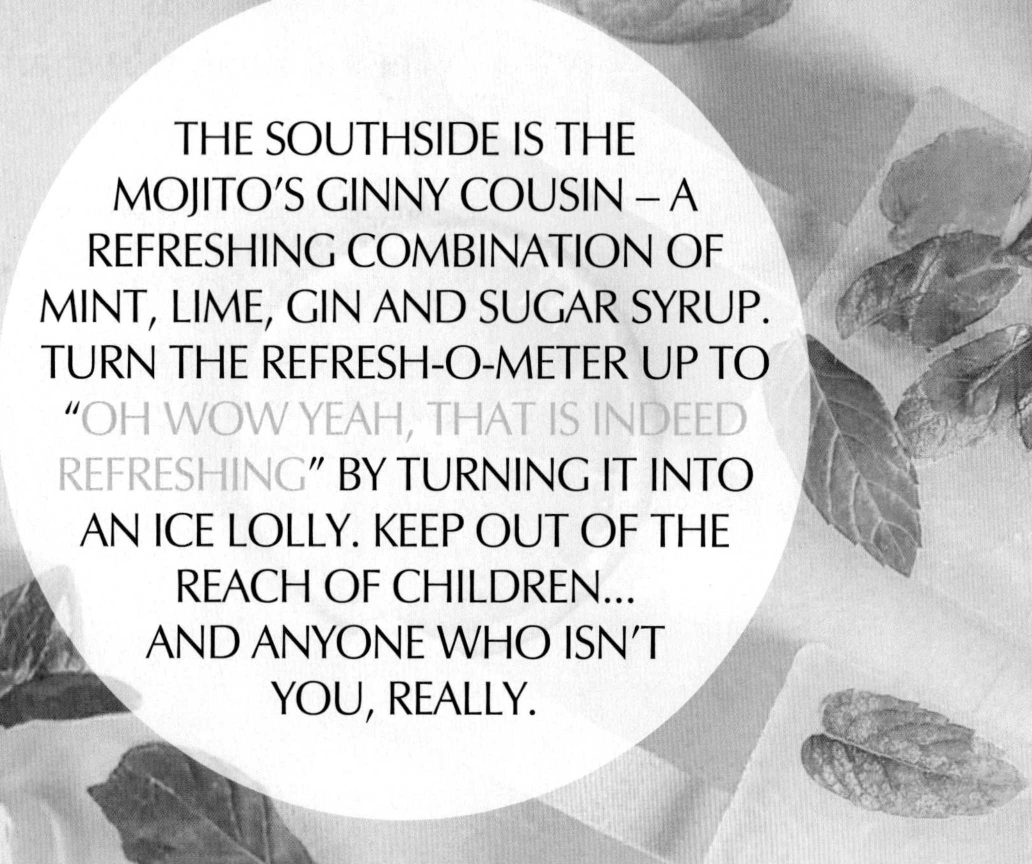

THE SOUTHSIDE IS THE MOJITO'S GINNY COUSIN – A REFRESHING COMBINATION OF MINT, LIME, GIN AND SUGAR SYRUP. TURN THE REFRESH-O-METER UP TO "OH WOW YEAH, THAT IS INDEED REFRESHING" BY TURNING IT INTO AN ICE LOLLY. KEEP OUT OF THE REACH OF CHILDREN... AND ANYONE WHO ISN'T YOU, REALLY.

Ice, Ice BABY

We guarantee your local ice cream van doesn't sell anything this delicious!

Recipe: KATHRYN HAWKINS
Picture: SHUTTERSTOCK

INGREDIENTS

- **100g caster sugar**
- **75ml gin**
- **Juice of 3-4 limes**
- **6-12 slices of fresh lime**
- **12-18 fresh mint leaves**

METHOD

1 Place the sugar and 100ml water in a saucepan over a low/medium heat until the sugar has dissolved – be careful not to let it boil. Leave to cool completely.

2 When cool, pour the syrup into a jug and add the lime juice and gin and stir well.

3 Take six 80ml lolly moulds and add a slice or two of lime and 2-3 mint leaves to each, then top up with the lolly mixture. Add the sticks and freeze until solid – overnight is best.

GIN & LIT

Words: JUDEY STRUTH

Read all about it! Gin's most memorable appearances in some of our favourite books...

Since gin's arrival on the social scene, her journey to the celeb she is today has been like some of her previous incarnations – a bit rough!

She dragged herself out of the gutters of 17th-century Britain and left her dubious beginnings behind.

She mixed coolly with the elite in Britain's colonies and brought pizzazz to many a cocktail party in '40s Manhattan, only to find herself out of favour again as the social tide turned.

She's gone from A-lister to the one nobody wants at their party.

But gin's star is in the ascendant once more.

And her sensational story can be charted through a series of cameos in some of our greatest works of literature...

1 James Bond is one of the smartest, smoothest and sexiest characters ever to grace the pages of a book. And the fact that he likes his gin only adds to his magnetism...

"A dry martini," Bond said. "One. In a deep Champagne goblet." "Oui, monsieur." "Just a moment. Three measures of Gordon's, one of vodka, half a measure of Kina Lillet. Shake it very well until it's ice-cold, then add a large thin slice of lemon peel. Got it?"
"Certainly, monsieur."
The barman seemed pleased with the idea.
"Gosh, that's certainly a drink," said Leiter.
Bond laughed. "When I'm… er… concentrating," he explained, "I never have more than one drink before dinner. But I do like that one to be large and very strong and very cold and very well-made. I hate small portions of anything, particularly when they taste bad. This drink's my own invention. I'm going to patent it when I can think of a good name."

Ian Fleming, Casino Royale

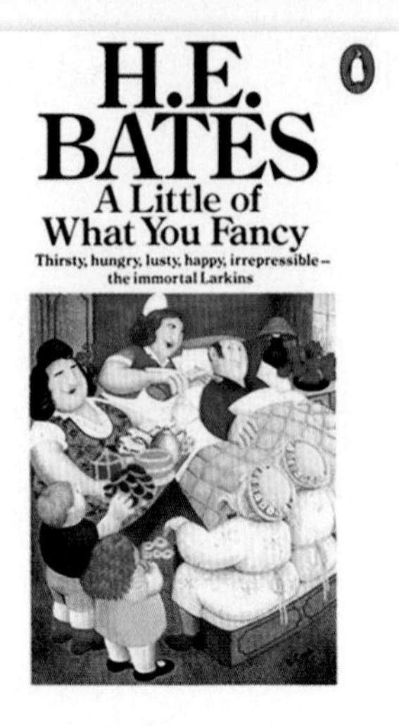

2 A snifter can be a boon in a difficult situation. Having just heard the terrible news that her beloved Pop Larkin is dead, Edith Pilchester dithers between the church and the Hare & Hounds. She plumps for the pub, but finds a pet jackdaw there that lets her combine drink and devotions.

"Gin," the hedge-cutter said. "Drop o' gin and 'e'll talk till the cows come home. Says the Lord's Prayer sometimes."
"Didn't I hear him," the butcher said, "say the 23rd Psalm once, too?"
"Two gins," the hedge-cutter said, "and 'e'll recite the whole of bloody Genesis."
At these words Miss Pilchester suddenly realised that the jackdaw hadn't even got its gin.
"Bring the poor thing its gin! Great God Almighty, we all need a drink sometimes, don't we?"

H.E. Bates, A Little Of What You Fancy

3 Albus Dumbledore is one of literature's greatest wizards. But when he goes to the orphanage to interview Tom Riddle, it's gin that works magic on the suspicious Matron...

Mrs Cole's eye fell upon a bottle of gin and two glasses that had certainly not been present a few seconds before. "Er – may I offer you a glass of gin?" she said in an extra-refined voice.
"Thank you very much," said Dumbledore, beaming.
It soon became clear that Mrs Cole was no novice when it came to gin drinking. Pouring them both a generous measure, she drained her own glass in one gulp. Smacking her lips frankly, she smiled at Dumbledore for the first time, and he didn't hesitate to press his advantage.

J.K. Rowling, Harry Potter And The Half-blood Prince

4 Victory Gin was Winston Smith's only means of escape from the horrors of 1984. Don't we wish we could give him a wee glass of Hendrick's or Monkey 47 to ease his pain!

The tears welled up in his eyes. A passing waiter noticed that his glass was empty and came back with the gin bottle. He took up his glass and sniffed at it. The stuff grew not less but more horrible with every mouthful he drank. But it had become the element he swam in. It was his life, his death, and his resurrection. It was gin that sank him into stupor every night, and gin that revived him every morning. When he woke, seldom before eleven hundred, it would have been impossible even to rise from the horizontal if it had not been for the bottle and teacup placed beside the bed overnight.

George Orwell, Nineteen Eighty-Four

5 A little drinkie can warm even the coldest heart, as Mr Bumble the beadle discovered. Fortunately for him, the effects were short-lived...

Mr Bumble walked on with long strides; and little Oliver, firmly grasping his gold-laced cuff, trotted beside him, enquiring at the end of every quarter of a mile whether they were "nearly there", to which interrogations Mr Bumble returned very brief and snappish replies; for the temporary blandness which gin and water awakens in some bosoms had by this time evaporated, and he was once again a beadle.

Charles Dickens, Oliver Twist

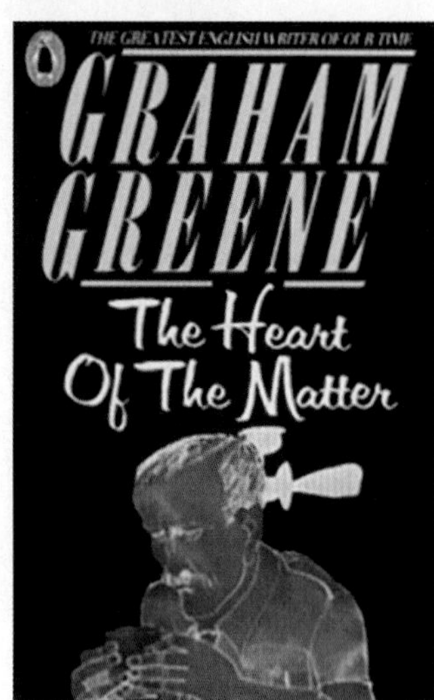

6 Recently arrived in West Africa, struggling in an alien environment, Wilson clutches at anything offering a taste of home and normality. Luckily, there is gin...

He couldn't tell that this was one of those occasions a man never forgets: a small cicatrice had been made on the memory, a wound that would ache whenever certain things combined – the taste of gin at mid-day, the smell of flowers under a balcony, the clang of corrugated iron.

Graham Greene, The Heart Of The Matter

7 Gerald Durrell recounts a night of abandoned drinking with a Cameroonian statesman. Had a tough week? Take your inspiration from the wise words of the Fon of Bafut.

The Fon surveyed the bottle gloomily. "Whisky done finish," he pointed out.
"Yes," I replied unhelpfully.
"Well," said the Fon, undaunted, "we go drink gin."

Gerald Durrell, A Zoo In My Luggage

Around The World In 80 GINS

Words: CLAIRE BARTLETT, LAURA BROWN, LESLEY MANUEL, KATRINA PATRICK, CARA SCOTT-MORRISON, JUDEY STRUTH, TRACEY STEEL, MAGGIE SWINBURNE

We took a whistle-stop tour across the globe in search of the very best gins... we even went to the moon!

Argentina

PRINCIPE DE LOS APOSTOLES MATE GIN

Yummy botanicals including peppermint, eucalyptus, pink grapefruit skin and yerba mate come together beautifully in Argentina's finest export since Lionel Messi.

apostolesgin.com

Australia

FOUR PILLARS SPICED NEGRONI GIN

A conversation between a distiller and a Sydney bar manager about creating the perfect gin for a Negroni resulted in Four Pillars Spiced. Using Tasmanian pepperberry leaf and lemon myrtle as base botanicals and adding cinnamon, Grains of Paradise and whole organic blood oranges, this gin is spicy and aromatic. It's quite unusual to use the whole fruit, but it's needed to support the heavy spices. After drinking this gin in a Negroni, we certainly needed a pillar or four to support us...

fourpillarsgin.com.au

Austria

BLUE GIN

Packed with a grand total of 27 herbs, spices and other botanicals on top of our pal juniper, Blue Gin packs the punch you'd expect from Austria's most decorated distiller, Hans Reisetbauer. Lemon and spice take the high notes, followed by delicious liquorice. This is "Around the World in 27 Botanicals", which fly in from Egypt, China, Macedonia, Romania, Turkey, Holland and Vietnam to name but a few.

bluegin.cc

Belgium

BUSS N° 509

Raspberry gin was the first in the BUSS N° 509 Author Collection and has been followed by pink grapefruit, Persian peach, White Rain and elderflower flavour variations. You don't need to be Poirot to work out that this is a treat for all gin enthusiasts and a wonderful foundation for anyone who likes to mix it up a bit.

bussspirits.com

Brazil

ARAPURU LONDON DRY GIN

Arapuru is a traditionally handmade London Dry gin with an unparalleled Brazilian twist. This versatile drink borrows its palate from the colours of the Amazonian Arapuru bird, that according to legend, brings luck and good fortune to whoever comes across it. The sunburst plumage is replicated in warming waves of cashew, cinnamon and a slightly orange zing. Arapuru is quite simply an Art Deco gem of Brazilian infused sophistication, perfect for a late summer's cocktail soiree.

arapuru.com.br

Canada

UNGAVA

This premium dry gin will appeal to the connoisseurs out there! It's a mellow beauty made with plants and berries of the tundra.

ungava-gin.com

Colombia

DICTADOR TREASURE AGED GIN

What makes this gin unique is its key ingredient, limon mandarino – a tangerine and lemon hybrid. This gives the gin a beautiful balance between acidity and sweetness. It's placed in aged oak barrels that have previously been used for rum, adding to the sweet notes of the tangerine and giving a very smooth finish. It also contributes to its slight amber colour. This citrusy gin certainly lives up to its name of Treasure.

dictador.com

Czech Republic

OMG: OH MY GIN

OMG doesn't boast any secret ingredient that can only be harvested by unicorn-riding mermaids once a year during the light of a full moon. This is simply an authentic distilled gin created with 16 herbs and spices by one man who loved the taste and wants to share it. Cheers to that!

zufanek.cz

Denmark

COPENHAGEN DIST. ORANGE GIN

This Danish distillery has created a fruity concoction that's a blend of rich oranges and bold juniper with a hint of allspice that brings warmth and prune that deepens the flavour palette. Complex and courageous but, when sipped neat, it delivers a truly satisfying bitter kick.

copenhagendistillery.com

VICTORIA'S RHUBARB GIN

Nothing says English summer more than rhubarb. This tart, fruity gin is made from a crop of rhubarb originally grown in the kitchen garden of Buckingham Palace during Victorian times. If you need us, we'll be in the garden languidly stirring our gin 'n' ginger with a stalk of rhubarb.

warneredwards.com

BROCKMANS

This is a gin to enjoy after dark, which happily means that during the British winter months, we can break open a bottle at 2.48pm. It's so intensely smooth you can drink it neat over ice without burning your throat or prickling your eyes. Seductive and suave, it's the James Bond of gins.

brockmansgin.com

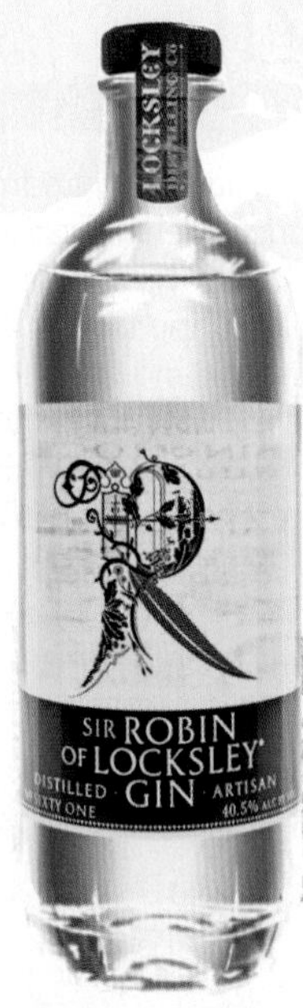

SIR ROBIN OF LOCKSLEY

Robin Hood, riding through the glen Robin Hood, Robin Hood, with his band of men. This is his gin, it's really good Robin Hood, Robin Hood, Robin Hood... Named after, you guessed it, Robin Hood, we'll be a band of merry men and women after a few of these.

locksleydistilling.com

GERANIUM GIN

Geranium Gin was created by a father-and-son team who drew on their knowledge of history to make what they dubbed "the best gin ever". Geranium and juniper make splendid bedfellows in this dry but aromatic gin that tastes great with tonics and sweet mixers alike.

geraniumgin.com

FOREST GIN

Only a few thousand bottles of this small batch, double, double gold-winning gin are produced each year and there's usually a wait. Get your name on the list and enjoy it over ice with Fever Tree Tonic, a twist of grapefruit peel and a sprig of fresh rosemary. Chin, chin!

forestgin.com

CHASE WILLIAMS SLOE GIN

Made lovingly in the Hertfordshire countryside, this has intense notes of sloe berries and juniper with a smooth mouth-feel and deep finish. Top up with posh tonic, fling in a slice of apple and channel Margot Channing in *All About Eve*, darling.

chasedistillery.co.uk

SILENT POOL

24 sultry botanicals make up this complex and mysterious gin. Pour over ice, add a dash of tonic and a twist of orange peel then enjoy.

silentpooldistillers.com

ONE GIN

This is an ethical gin distilled from 10 different botanicals from across the globe. Sage provides a unique flavour profile, and the genus name of the sage plant is derived from the Latin word "salvare" which means "save". One's vision is to help an estimated 663 million people worldwide by funding projects to help parts of the world's population without access to clean water. A well-rounded gin with a life-changing goal.

onedifference.org

HIDDEN CURIOSITIES

There's nothing hidden about the charms of this multi-award winning small batch artisan gin. Distilled in the Surrey Hills and handcrafted with 20 botanicals, its quality and flavour are to be found from the very first sip.

hiddencuriosities.com

Estonia

CRAFTER'S DRY GIN

This handcrafted London gin from Estonia was recently awarded a gold medal at the International Alcohol Awards Competition in California. Made from local wheat and the botanicals veronica and fennel, it's the result of many experiments with locally-sourced ingredients. Produced using the traditional pot still method in an authentic last-century copper vat, and bottled in a distinctive royal blue bottle (which has also won an award for design), this is refreshingly dry gin.

liviko.ee

Finland

KYRO NAPUE

Locally foraged botanicals like meadowsweet, sea buckthorn, cranberries and birch leaves unite in this rye-based gin. It conjures up early mornings frolicking through a Finnish meadow – something we're sure you've had plenty experience of doing, lord knows we have. Voted The World's Best Gin for Gin & Tonic in the past, we like ours with plenty of ice, a stick of rosemary, a handful of cranberries and Fever Tree tonic.

kyrodistillery.com

France

GABRIEL BOUDIER

Gabriel Boudier is famous for its vast array of liqueurs and cremes de fruits, but it's their saffron gin that's found a place in our drinks cabinet. The recipe was discovered in the Boudier archives, and celebrates English gin, Indian spices and French know-how. As anyone who's been on holiday to Spain and panic-bought a thimble-sized container of four saffron for 25 in the airport knows, it's one of the world's most expensive spices – but this gin is a remarkably reasonably-priced bottle of amber gorgeousness.

boudier.com

Germany

THE BITTER TRUTH

There's a whole world of delicious at The Bitter Truth – unusual drops and dashes, spiced bitters and gorgeous liqueurs – and their Pink Gin is no exception. Originally invented by sailors as a sea sickness cure, the smooth blend of craft gin and aromatic bitters certainly floats our boat. It's spicy and floral with distinct notes of liquorice, fennel and caraway. We may need to book a cruise so we can properly test it out, but failing that, try it in a martini cocktail or on the rocks with a dash of fresh lemon juice.

the-bitter-truth.com

MONKEY 47

Monkey gin is made with 47 botanicals, including sweet and sour cranberries, before it's matured in traditional earthenware vessels. This is not what you would call a traditional gin, but we would strongly recommend you taste and try. Our tester went ape for it!

monkey47.com

SKIN GIN

If you're looking for something a bit different to your traditional, juniper-centric gins, then this is the tipple for you. The Moroccan mint and Vietnamese coriander create a fresh yet earthy base, while the grapefruit, orange and lime follow nicely on the palate, resulting in a deceptively light and refreshing gin. Skin Gin actively encourage consumers to judge their gin by its bottle, creating beautiful leather-clad bottles that just scream quality. This is a gin that demands pride of place on your trolley. You can even design your own branded bottle, picking from an astounding 500 colour and surface varieties. Minimum order values apply, however, so you'll need to bulk-buy. Lifetime's supply of bespoke bottles? Sure.

skin-gin.com

Greece

GRACE GIN

Grace Gin is the delicious result of the shared vision of three spirited Greek women. It's made using rock samphire that can only be gathered during May and June, as well as myrtle and orange blossom, picked by the distillery's very own Three Graces from the surrounding orange trees. Their secret ingredient? Meraki, the Greek word for putting your heart and soul into something.

lkc-drinks.com

Greenland

ISFJORD PREMIUM ARCTIC GIN

A beautiful blend of 12 different botanicals and distilled with Greenlandic iceberg water, ISFJORD truly lives up to its moniker of Premium Arctic Gin. It's a fresh and fruity gin, filled with juniper berries and a bittersweet orange zest. A hint of spice comes through from the cardamom, balancing out the flavours and making this an incredibly smooth drink overall. Enjoy with crushed ice, your tonic of choice, a slice of orange to finish, and a soundtrack of Björk.

isfjord.com

Iceland

VOR PREMIUM GIN

VOR is the Icelandic word for spring, where the inspiration for this gin comes from – the sharp, invigorating taste of an Icelandic spring, melting into summer. It's non chill filtered to preserve the magical glacial haze that emerges when tonic is added.
VOR is packed full of botanicals that only grow in sub-Arctic regions and that you're unlikely to find anywhere else. Wild Icelandic juniper, crowberries and Iceland moss add subtle, lighter notes to the robust character of VOR's base spirit, which comes from 100% Icelandic barley. This gin is a refreshing glass of pure, unadulterated Iceland.

vorgin.is

India

BLUE RIBAND

Not to be confused with one of Britain's favourite biscuits, this is the bestselling gin in India. Juniper, citrus and spice combine for a peppery but smooth gin. We preferred it in a martini rather than with the traditional tonic, so grab your olives.

goencho.in

Ireland

EXILES

This superior Irish gin is the only gin in the world using the symbol of Ireland, the shamrock, as a botanical. Traditional, classic gin from a family who have been distilling for 300 years. Sláinte!

BERTHA'S REVENGE

Using whey alcohol from dairy farmers in Cork and named after the world's oldest cow, Big Bertha, this milk gin is a sweet mouthful of cardamom, cloves and cinnamon.

ballyvolanespirits.ie

The Islands

HARRIS // ISLE OF HARRIS GIN

This gin has got it all going on. Bitter orange, lime and grapefruit spiced with coriander, pepper and vanilla develop into complex rose, gooseberry and crushed herbs. All the flavours mingle beautifully with the star ingredient, sugar kelp, which adds notes of the sea. Refreshing and dry, Isle of Harris is best enjoyed with tonic, a dash of sugar kelp aromatic water and a red grapefruit wedge. Sip slowly and feel yourself float away on a wave of gin bliss.

---

harrisdistillery.com

ISLAY // THE BOTANIST

Nine classic gin botanicals are blended with 22 hand-picked local ingredients from the Isle of Islay. The mix is then slow-distilled at low-pressure in an old pot-still called Ugly Betty, producing a smooth and complex floral gin. There's nothing ugly about the rich and mellow results. We're going a bit fancy and trying it with the Thomas Henry Cherry Blossom tonic and an oh-so-'70s cherry on a stick.

---

thebotanist.com

JERSEY // ROYAL MARE

Made from the finest Jersey Royal potato spirit on the La Mare Wine estate, Royal Gin is pretty special. Infused with seven gin botanicals and delicate elderflower from the estate, then double-distilled to create a subtle and balanced flavour. We're sticking with tradition at *The Joy Of Gin* and serving it over ice with Goldberg tonic and a simple sprig of mint. Sadly, La Mare Royal Gin can't be posted, so we'll all need to go on holiday to Jersey to buy a bottle. While we're there we can drive around in a burgundy Triumph Roadster and solve crimes, the sound of a reggae accordion following us everywhere we go. No, wait a minute, we've got ourselves confused with Bergerac. This happens a lot.

---

lamarewineestate.com

ISLES OF SCILLY // WESTWARD FARMS

We're spoiled for choice with these three distinctive gins. Only 28 bottles are produced on a single run, so each small batch is truly unique in flavour. For vibrant citrus and pepper, pick Scilly Gin served with tonic. For something different, Wild Wingletang is infused with gorse blossom to produce green, nutty notes – experience all the aromas by serving straight over ice. If you love florals, you can't beat the Rose Geranium – made from geranium extract produced on the farm and blended with the Scilly Gin. Lovely with lemon and the sandy beaches of Scilly in your sights.

westwardfarm.co.uk

SHETLAND // SHETLAND REEL

Produced at Saxa Vord distillery in Unst, the most northerly in the UK, this is a traditional style gin with a Shetland twist. Locally grown apple mint is added to botanicals that include coriander, cassia bark and orris. The award-winning result is light and refreshing with a dry edge. Adding tonic really brings out the fruitiness, but this is our go-to gin for a Negroni. It's the perfect cocktail to show off the bright, sweet notes of Shetland Reel. One too many, though, and you'll be dancing a Shetland Reel.

shetlandreel.com

ISLE OF WIGHT // MERMAIDS

WARNING: Drinking this will turn you into a real mermaid!*

Full of island flavours, this gin is bursting with botanicals and fresh ingredients including hops, English coriander, elderflower, and rock samphire hand-picked from a secret cliff-side location (how mysterious!). And then it takes time to make – a day of steeping, a day of distilling and seven days of rest to allow the flavours to marry perfectly. The result? A smooth, citrusy, peppery gin.

*Are we lying? You'll have to drink it to find out!

isleofwightdistillery.com

Israel

AKKO

Akko is the first gin in the world to be made only from Israeli plants – 12 botanicals that grow in Galilee. Made in a distillery on the ruins of Tel Mimas, a renowned wine-growing region in antiquity, Akko's base spirit is made of grapes. This is a well-rounded, aromatic gin that celebrates the region's landscape and traditions.

jullius.com

Italy

GIN DEL PROFESSORE MADAME

Just like Madame on the bottle, this fruity gin is mysterious and magnetising thanks to its mix of turmeric, cinnamon, tansy and more. You'll be longing for a second date.

distilleriaquaglia.it

GIN DEL PROFESSORE MONSIEUR

Madame's dapper consort is heavy on the juniper and the suave. But we blame him for the rise in competitive moustache growing and the surge in public facial hair grooming.

distilleriaquaglia.it

MALFY

This is a gorgeous gin with lemon and citrus notes that give it a summertime kick in your glass.

malfygin.com

BOTTEGA BACUR GIN

Would our heads be turned by posh gin in a swanky copper bottle? Of course they would – especially when it tastes as good as this. Crafted by historic Italian distiller Bottega, Bacur includes locally sourced botanicals from the Veneto region of Italy. Alpine juniper, myrtle, sage marry with sharp lemon zest and perfumed spices. It makes us want to run across a chamomile lawn or skip in a wild flower meadow while clutching a gin and elderflower fizz (both quite hard to achieve without spillage).

bottegaspa.com

Japan

KI NO BI

Made at The Kyoto Distillery from creamy, sweet Japanese rice grain spirit, the traditional base for sake, and precision blended with eleven botanicals for a delicate and well-balanced dry gin. The juniper complements the locally sourced botanicals – fresh yuzu with a sansho pepper thread, gyokuro tea, pine scented hinoki wood and a warming, spicy ginger root finish. We love serving KI NO BI sake-style with hot water and imagining ourselves in a faraway land, or at least somewhere that's not our sofa.

kyotodistillery.jp

Liechtenstein

TELSER DRY GIN

A mere 11 botanical are used to give this multi-award-winning small batch gin its character – juniper, coriander, angelica root, cinnamon, ginger, zinto shell, bitter orange, curaçao orange, chamomile, lavender and elderberry blossoms. Distiller Marcel Telser was the first German-speaking member of The Gin Guild in London, so safe to say he knows how to make a great gin.

telserdistillery.com

Luxembourg

DRY GIN 28

Five generations of master distillers has brought you Dry Gin 28 by Filliers. Juniper berries from Italy, orange blossom from Spain and bitter root from India are just some of the exotic ingredients.

filliersdrygin28.com

Madeira

FIRST GIN

An island with no gin! What a scandal, especially when you consider that juniper is native to Madeira. They've rectified the situation with the appropriately-named First Gin, flavoured with local botanicals and sugarcane.

firstgin.pt

Mexico

MEZCAL

Put that tequila to once side and delve into Mezcal Gin, a small-batch handcrafted spirit that brings together the complex flavours of artisanal mezcal with the freshness and perfume of gin.

mezcalgin.com.mx

The Moon

MOONSHOT GIN

That Boutique-y Gin Company, for reasons unknown, send the botanicals for Moonshot Gin to the edge of space before vacuum distilling them when they touch back down on our fine planet. They also stick a bit of moon rock into the mix for good measure, because why on earth not? It's out of this world.

thatboutiqueygincompany.com

The Netherlands

DUTCH COURAGE

Nine botanicals from all over the world collide in this award-winning gin from the Zuidam family distillery. Whole fresh lemons and sweet orange amp up the citrus notes, followed by earthy juniper and a hint of spice and vanilla. When cocktail hour awaits, the balance of Dutch Courage makes a perfect Dry Martini.

zuidam.eu

New Zealand

LIGHTHOUSE GIN

Inspired by the spectacular Cape Palliser Lighthouse on the southernmost tip of the North Island of New Zealand, each bottle of Lighthouse Gin contains a unique blend of botanicals, including fresh zest from New Zealand Navel oranges and Yen Ben lemons.

lighthousegin.co.nz

SCRAPEGRACE

Twelve botanicals, water from New Zealand's Southern Alps and a whisky still combine to make this gin an absolute must for your collection.

scapegracegin.com

BLACK ROBIN GIN

This contemporary London Dry gin is inspired by the critically endangered Chatham Island's Black Robin with a donation from each bottle sold given to he Royal Forest and Bird Society of New Zealand. Classy and conscientious.

blackrobingin.co.nz

Northern Ireland

ECHLINVILLE

This delightful little number is made in pot stills at the Echlinville distillery in County Down using barley grown on the distillery farm, and botanicals including whin bush petals and Strangford Lough seaweed. It was produced in honour of their namesake, Captain Charles Echlin, and if you ask us, he should be very proud!

echlinville.com

BOATYARD DOUBLE GIN

The Boatyard Distillery is the first working (legal) distillery in Fermanagh since 1887. Their delicious organic gin goes through a double distillation process, hence the name. Spicy and refreshing, it's a perfect base for cocktails. The bottle's a work of art, too.

boatyarddistillery.com

SHORTCROSS GIN

Created to be a classical gin with a unique twist, Shortcross is made with locally-foraged clover, elderflower and elderberries, as well as apples grown nearby. We love a craft gin (have you noticed?) and the Rademon Estate is proud to be Northern Ireland's first award-winning craft distillery.

shortcrossgin.com

Norway

KIMERUD DISTILLED GIN

Only one year into its production, Kimerud Gin received the highest award from 120 of the world's top sommeliers and chefs... and we can see why! The heritage and geography of Norway adds to the quality of this gin, blending hand-picked botanicals popular in the Viking era including ginger root, lemon peel, walnut and Rhodiola Rosea. This final ingredient is collected from the cliffs in the north of Norway. This slightly herby gin is strong but smooth – and if it's good enough for Vikings, it's good enough for us. Please ready our longship, we are ready for a sea battle.

kimerud.no

HARAHORN

Inspired by a mythical horned hare and named after a Norwegian mountain, Harahorn is a potent gin wrapped up in a very pretty bottle. Blueberries, rhubarb, juniper, marjoram and bladderwrack from around the country give this small batch gin (only 400 litres are produced at a time) a distinctly Nordic flavour. We topped ours up with ginger ale and threw in some fresh blueberries, and we were very pleased with ourselves indeed.

detnorskebrenneri.no

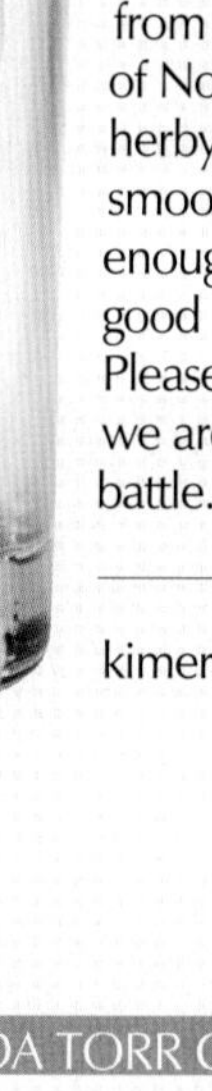

VIDDA TORR GIN

Think Norway and think of fresh pine forests, alpine flower meadows, mountain lakes and Morten Harket from A-ha. All of these things feature in this delicious gin. The impressive list of botanicals includes heather, yarrow, chamomile, meadowsweet and pine shoots amongst many others. All are local to Norway and some are even foraged by the head distiller himself. This gin has a piny nose with florals adding sweetness and a certain delicacy. "Vidda" means "mountain plateau" which is definitely where you are transported after your first sip. (We made up the bit about A-ha. No Mortens were harmed in the making of this gin.)

oslohd.co.uk

Panama

GIN CABALLITO

Made from extra neutral alcohol from sugarcane honey and a mixture of sweeteners, this intriguing extra-dry tipple has typical citrus and juniper flavours. It's Panama's most popular gin.

varelahermanos.com

Peru

GIN'CA PERUVIAN DRY GIN

GIN'CA is the first Peruvian premium gin — four-times distilled with the purest sugar cane spirit and 11 botanicals from small local producers. It's a labour of love: the citrus fruits are peeled by hand, one by one, the peppers and the juniper berries are crushed by hand, and each leaf of huacatay, rosemary, and verbena is removed individually… you guessed it, by hand.

tid.pe

Philippines

GINEBRA SAN MIGUEL

You're probably familiar with the Filipino beer, San Miguel, but have you heard of San Miguel gin? A subsidiary of the same company, Ginebra San Miguel is the number one selling gin in the world, thanks in no small part to the insane popularity of gin in the Philippines (there's even a dedicated word for a gin drinking session: ginuman). In production for over 180 years, Ginebra San Miguel is a classic Dutch-type gin, with lasting juniper notes. Often enjoyed with ice and pineapple juice, this simple drink is cheap and cheerful, hence its overwhelming popularity. If bagging nine Gold Quality Labels from the Monde Selection isn't impressive enough, Ginebra San Miguel also own one of the most popular Filipino basketball teams, The Gin Kings, Barangay Ginebra San Miguel. Talk about a slam-dunk success.

ginebrasan
miguel.com

Portugal

SHARISH BLUE MAGIC

Sharish Blue Magic is exactly that. Magic. Not only does it owe its mesmerisingly unique blue hue to a flower known as the butterfly pea, but it also undertakes a metamorphosis of its own, transforming into a glorious pink when mixed with tonic. A bit like that Global Hypercolor T-shirt you owned in the '90s. It would be easy to pass Sharish Blue Magic off as a gimmick gin, but you'd be mistaken for doing so. Beyond the colour lies a wonderfully refreshing fruity flavour, packed with summer berries and citrus traces. Underpinned by notes of cinnamon and vanilla, Blue Magic is perfect served with tonic and a slice of apple.

sharishgin.com

FRIDAY CHIC GIN

This floral gin is produced by Cavas da Montanha, a family business from the Bairrada wine region in Portugal. Being from a wine region, the use of vine leaves as one of four botanicals is no surprise, but the combination of mango, passion fruit and papaya is. It gives the gin a beautiful freshness like the most delicious fruit salad. With cardamom, orange blossom and juniper as the other elements it all combines to produce a very smooth drink. Chic by name, chic by nature.

facebook.com/fridaychicgin

Russia

POLUGAR NO. 10

Polugar No. 10, produced by Rodinov & Sons, uses a classic recipe that belonged to Russian nobility of the 19th Century. It contains cloudberry, lingonberry, calamus, 12 secret Siberian herbs and roots, and the end result is a gin that has notes of traces of baked bread, honey, field flowers and home-made pastries.

russiandistiller.com

Scotland

ROCK ROSE

This clean, floral and surprisingly fruity gin comes from Dunnet Bay Distillers in Caithness with a host of awards under its belt. It's named after one of its 18 botanicals, rhodiola rosea, which grows on the cliffs near the distillery. Raiding Vikings harvested it to give them extra strength for continuing their arduous journeys, and while the distillers themselves make no claims about the strength-giving properties of their gin – why run the risk?

dunnetbaydistillers.co.uk

DUNDEE GIN CLASSIC DRY

The Dundee Gin Company was founded in 2017 and have enjoyed huge success with their classic dry gin. Taking 10 botanicals from all over the world, this gin combines them to create a smooth and well-rounded drink with a lovely little spicy kick at the end. This spiciness comes from the use of liquorice root from the Mediterranean, ground nutmeg from the West Indies and cinnamon bark from Madagascar, all distilled with the smooth and fresh waters from the rolling hills around Dundee. This sophisticated, cosmopolitan creation puts Bonnie Dundee squarely on the global gin map. Jute, jam, journalism... and juniper.

thedundeegin.com

STIRLING GIN

From humble beginnings in a Scottish kitchen, Stirling Gin has fast become a local leader, in taste, quality and popularity. Making use of locally foraged nettles, Stirling Gin indulges a unique blend of botanicals to produce a deliciously classic drink. Pair with torn basil for a vibrant gin experience.

stirlinggin.co.uk

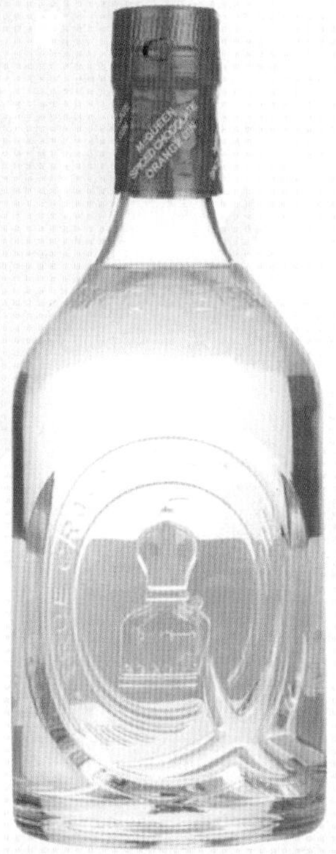

MCQUEEN SPICED CHOC ORANGE GIN

Dear Santa, if you're reading: we don't want a Terry's Chocolate Orange in the toe of our stocking this Christmas. We'd much prefer a bottle of McQueen Spiced Chocolate Orange gin instead. While you're there, you might as well pick us up a bottle of their Chocolate Mint gin, too. We promise we've been exceptionally good this year (so far).

masterofmalt.com

PARTRIDGES

World-famous London store Partridges has launched its delicious Chelsea Flower Show Gin – but why on earth is this very English-sounding concoction lurking in the Scotland section? It's made in collaboration with Dunnet Bay Distillers, that's why. It contains rose petals and marigold for a suitably floral celebration of one of the world's most iconic flower shows.

partridges.co.uk

Singapore

PAPER LANTERN SICHUAN PEPPER GIN

Founded by husband-and-wife duo, Rick Ames and Simin Kayhan Ames, Paper Lantern Distilling's story is as interesting and unique as the gin itself. After moving to Singapore and noticing a distinct lack of local spirits behind the bars, the one-time beer brewers and all-round spirit enthusiasts set about creating a craft gin that really showcased south-east Asian flavours. Just as paper lanterns mark the beginning of a new chapter, Paper Lantern Distilling marked a new chapter for Rick and Simin, as they raised an astounding $15,000 in just 30 hours, allowing them to crowdfund the first batch of their Thai rice-built, Sichuan Pepper Gin. Distilled with a unique blend of Asian botanicals, Sichuan Pepper is an aromatic delight, boasting distinctive citrus high notes, offset by spicy peppercorns, ginger and galangal. With a subtly sweet Thai honey finish, this really is a lovely warming gin, which despite its depth of flavour, is surprisingly light.

drinkpaperlantern.com

South Africa

HOPE CRAFT GINS

Hope On Hopkins has a trio of delights. London Dry Gin, Salt River and Mediterranean are all distilled in the very heart of Cape Town.

hopedistillery.co.za

Spain

GIN MARE

There's never been a better time to embrace the Spanish gintonic trend. This unusual blend contains the finest Mediterranean ingredients – Arbequina olives, thyme, basil, rosemary and mandarin sit alongside the traditional juniper and spice flavours. Go for the full experience with a traditional balloon glass and serve your gin over ice with a dash of fresh lemon and sprig of rosemary.

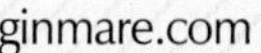

ginmare.com

SANTAMANIA GIN

This gin is named after the Spanish term for obsessive and, given that Spain has the highest consumption of gin in the world, the name fits. Unusually, the base ingredient for Santamania is grapes which makes the gin very smooth and gives it character. Amongst its many ingredients are Spanish pistachio nuts, raspberries, angelica and liquorice root. Their obsession pays off as this is a delicious, layered gin, and we like it best on the rocks.

destileria.madrid

Sweden

SPIRIT OF HVEN GIN

Handcrafted on the tiny island of Hven in the strait of Oresund, this lovely organic gin has nailed the clean taste of Scandinavia. Produced in small copper pot stills then oak matured to develop the botanical flavours. Look out for citrus, juniper and grains of paradise set with vanilla, pepper and spice. We like this gin with tonic, our frozen berry ice cubes and a few peppercorns, served in a massive glass. For those brave enough to try something stronger, there's also limited release Navy Strength gin.

hven.com

HERNÖ OLD TOM GIN

Founded in 2011 on the stunning Swedish High Coast, Hernö Gin has amassed an astounding number of awards. With a touch of honey and an extra helping of meadowsweet, Old Tom is smoother than its Hernö counterparts. Floral notes and a long-lasting juniper finish help create a bright and balanced gin. This modern take on the 18th century prohibited "Old Tom" gin (where the illegal beverage was dispensed from wooden black cats hung outside of pubs) is quite frankly, the cat's pyjamas.

hernogin.com

Switzerland

XELLENT SWISS EDELWEISS GIN

This cool character is distilled in copper alembics and uses fresh glacier water from Titlis. One too many and we guarantee you'll start singing Edelweiss from *The Sound Of Music.*

xellent.ch

Thailand

IRON BALLS GIN

"You always have options if you have balls" is the, er, interesting mantra of this particular gin – and it certainly has those! While most gin-based spirit is made from grain, Iron Balls ferment and distil pineapples and coconuts to make their base spirit, before re-distilling with ginger and lemongrass botanicals. The result is a fruity and quintessentially Thai gin that is about as far as you can get from your classic juniper-distilled grain spirit.

ironballsgin.com

USA

DEATH'S DOOR

This American craft gin from Washington Island, Wisconsin, has a surprisingly simple botanical mix of juniper berries, coriander and fennel. All the ingredients are sourced close to home, including wild island juniper, then distilled with local red winter wheat spirit. All the flavours come through – juniper up front, then spicy coriander and a cool fennel finish. Keep the serve simple to enjoy this soft, smooth gin at its best – try on the rocks or in a martini.

masterofmalt.com

Venezuela

WELLINGTON GIN

This American craft gin from Washington Island, Wisconsin, has a surprisingly simple botanical mix of juniper berries, coriander and fennel. All the ingredients are sourced close to home, including wild island juniper, then distilled with local red winter wheat spirit.
All the flavours come through – juniper up front, then spicy coriander and a cool fennel finish. Keep the serve simple to enjoy this soft, smooth gin.

dusa.com.ve

Wales

POLLINATION GIN

Pollination uses 29 different botanicals – 19 of which are foraged from the Snowdonia foothills, the Dyfi Forest, and the estuary marshlands. A very Welsh riot of chamomile, lemon balm, rowan berry and bramble, with local spring water, it's produced in limited batches of 100 bottles to respect the seasonality. It's a celebration of the local countryside, and the taste is unmistakably, wildly Wales.

dyfidistillery.com

DÀ MHÌLE SEAWEED GIN

Launched on St David's Day, this aromatic gin is made with handpicked seaweed from the Celtic coast. It's infused for three weeks, giving it a lovely light green hue before being triple-filtered and bottled.

damhile.co.uk

May Contain GIN

Words: CLAIRE BARTLETT

Ten things to do with gin… aside from drinking it, that is!

Crusty Pies

Boffins would tell you something dull about ethanol and gluten formation right about now… but we're no scientists! All we know is pie + gin = flaky pastry heaven!

Aftershave

Rather than reaching for your usual aftershave, a splash of gin will tighten the skin whilst cleaning out any nicks. Or you can be mega-fancy and buy Penhaligon's Juniper Sling eau de toilette, £175.

Red Wine Stains

Forget white wine – the higher alcohol percentage in gin will shift a red wine stain more effectively. Prevention is better than cure, though: if you'd been drinking gin in the first place, those stains would never have happened!

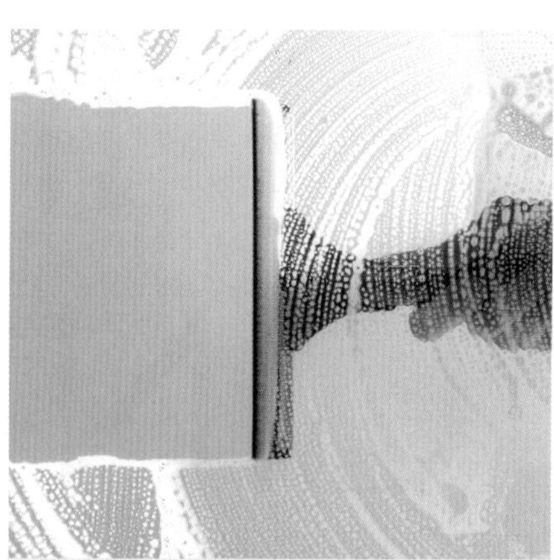

Washing Windows

For streak-free windows, spray them with gin and clean with a piece of silk. If you don't have any silk hanging around – and why ever not?! – use a clean, lint-free cloth instead.

Pickling Ingredient

It's not just humans who get pickled with gin – it's also brilliant for pickling cucumber! Fire up the barbecue – your burger just got fancy!

Shoe Deodoriser

Funky feet, no more! Spray some gin into the offending footwear to kill the odour-causing bacteria – or at least give them the hangover from hell.

Air Freshener

Add some water and a few drops of essential oil to gin (maybe not your best stuff) to a spray bottle to make the ultimate de-stinking cocktail.

Alleviating Arthritis Pain

Soaking golden raisins in gin for a week then eating 10 a day could ease arthritic pain. Juniper contains anti-inflammatory compounds as do the golden raisins. This is our kind of alternative remedy!

Cleaning Jewellery

Soaking your jewellery in gin makes it sparkle. Grab a soft toothbrush and a slug of gin and gently buff those jewels until they shine – we recommend you use Bombay Sapphire.

Mouthwash

After a swoosh around your mouth with a glug of gin, those cavity-causing bacteria will feel exactly the same way you do after several G&Ts. Emergencies only, otherwise your dentist will cry.

Images: SHUTTERSTOCK

Inspiring GIN-TERIORS!

Create your own sophisticated gin palace at home with luxe furnishings, metallic touches and rich tones

RECREATE the regal ambiance of a gin palace at home with a mix of stylish décor and metallic accents that evoke the charm and sophistication of the beloved spirit.

Choose a bar cart with a metallic frame in gold or chrome – turn over the page for more tips on that. Glass or marble surfaces complement these finishes beautifully, adding a touch of elegance. Incorporate decorative elements like metallic trays, coasters and a statement mirror to complete the luxurious atmosphere.

Deep, rich hues like teal, navy blue or burgundy are ideal for soft furnishings to provide a striking contrast to your glassware and metal.

If you get the blend right, your gin palace will exude opulence and become a stunning feature in the home.

BRUNING VELVET BARREL CHAIR, £109.99, wayfair.co.uk

TROPICAL LEAF TEAL CUSHION COVER, £12, Dunelm

DECORATIVE FLOWER ORNAMENT, £16, Next

BLANTON 2-PIECE NEST OF TABLES, £66.99,

VONSHEF HAMMERED STAINLESS STEEL ICE BUCKET, £24.99, wayfair.co.uk

CHENILLE THROW IN TEAL BLUE, £14.40, Habitat

KENTIA PALM, £75 in **DALSTON CHARCOAL LARGE POT,** £50, leafenvy.co.uk

OCTAGON SERVING TRAY, £38, John Lewis

LED BOTTLE LIGHTS, £3, HobbyCraft

Turn empty gin bottles into show-stopping table lamps

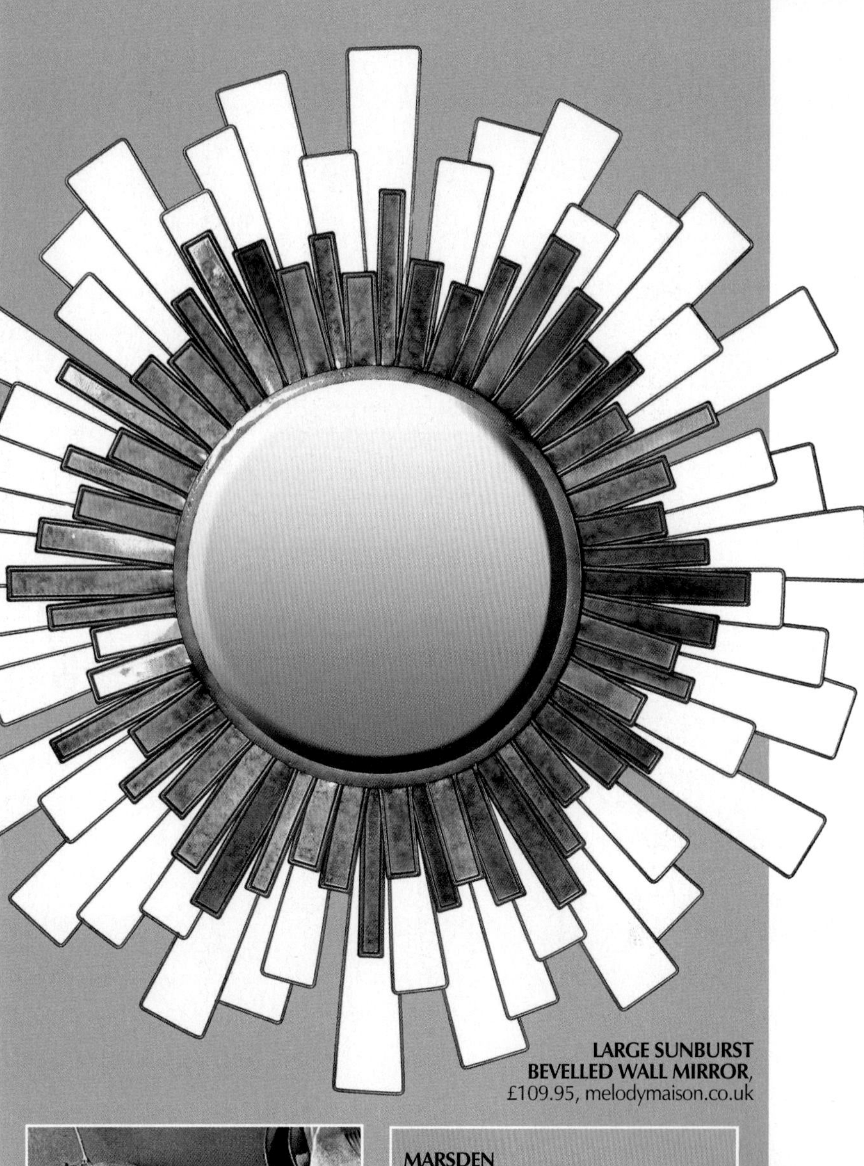

LARGE SUNBURST BEVELLED WALL MIRROR, £109.95, melodymaison.co.uk

DIABLO MARBLE SILVER CUSHION, £16, Dunelm

Set of two

SET OF 2 ABDULJALIL BAR STOOLS, £119.99, wayfair.co.uk

NATURAL MANGO WOOD SERVING BOARD, £28, Next

MARSDEN INDUSTRIAL HOOP ANTIQUE BRASS 6-LIGHT CEILING LIGHT, £135, Dunelm

Turn over to create your ultimate bar cart...

METALLIC GOLD COASTERS, £12.99, The Range

SET OF 2 CLEAR, ANGULAR GIN GLASSES, £15, Next

Words: KATRINA PATRICK ALL PRICE CORRECT AT TIME OF GOING TO PRESS

Get TROLLIED!

How to stock the ultimate bar cart...

Step 1: Build A Base

Stock up on your core collection – we're talking vodka, gin, rum, tequila, whisky and vermouth. Don't get charmed by novelty flavoured liquors that will collect dust for the next few years. Anchovy and lime infused vodka? Behave.

Step 2: Choose Your Plus Ones

Having the main ingredients of your favourite cocktails to hand will prevent the old throw-it-in-and-see-what-happens effort that inevitably ends in disappointment. Try triple sec, bitters, tonic water, ginger ale, and tomato juice to get you started.

Step 3: Get Hands On

Muddler, strainer, corkscrew and jigger may all sound like wrestling moves, but honing your craft with just these four tools will take your cocktails from novice to knock-out in one round.

Step 4: Infuse Your Personality

Put your stamp on your cocktail trolley with swizzle sticks, flowers, napkins, coasters and prints to finish the look.

ANTIQUE SILVER/CHAMPAGNE ART DECO DRINKS TROLLEY, £199, www.margoandplum.co.uk

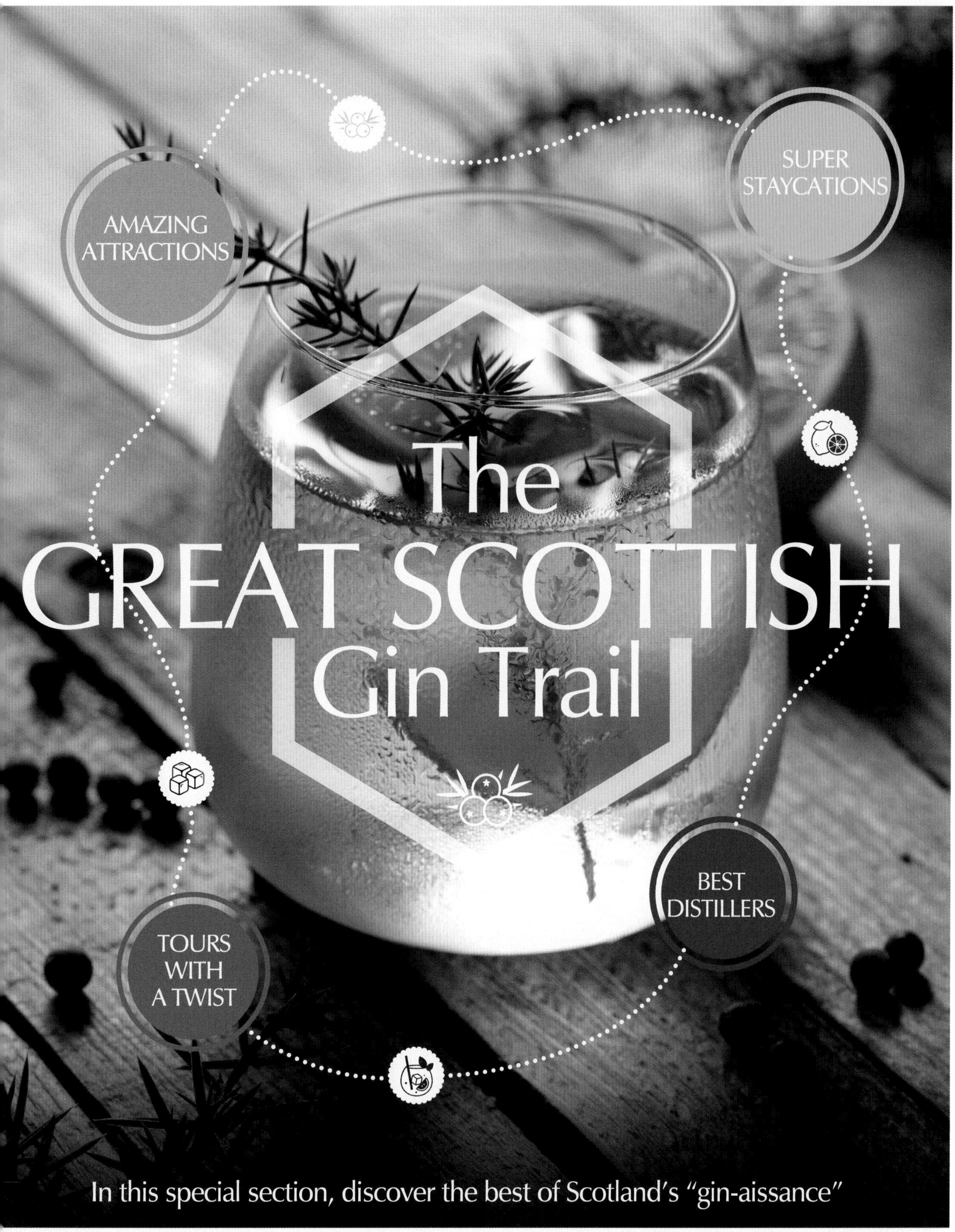

The GREAT SCOTTISH Gin Trail

In this special section, discover the best of Scotland's "gin-aissance"

SCOTTISH gin production has seen a meteoric rise in the past 20 years. In 2000, there were only two gins distilled in Scotland – Tanqueray from Cameronbridge in Fife and Hendrick's from William Grant & Sons in Girvan.

But, since then, distilleries have been quietly popping up across the country. Now there are around 100, producing gins of every strength and flavour you could imagine.

And this so-called "ginaissance" shows no sign of abating. Each gin is as distinctive as the gorgeous Scottish landscape that surrounds its distillery – no tour is the same, and each one gives you a unique perspective and flavour of the land itself.

With all this in mind, we've decided to take a deep dive into all that Scotland's burgeoning gin sector has to offer. Split across five regional sections, we've spoken to distillers, visited bars and rounded up the best attractions and places to stay.

So please, come join us on The Great Scottish Gin Trail...

South Breakwater, Aberdeen

North-East

Breathtaking beaches and artisan gin distilleries lie in wait along Scotland's cold shoulder and the far north coast, protected by rugged cliffs and sentinel castles

THE north-east of Scotland has many claims to fame, and now artisan gin has been added to its enviable list of exports.

Speyside is Scotland's whisky capital, with more than half of the country's distilleries. Aberdeen Angus cows produce some of the world's best beef, and Royal Deeside is the home of Balmoral Castle, beloved by Queen Victoria.

The north-east, stretching up Scotland's east coast from south of Aberdeen and beyond Inverness to Thurso, is also home to more castles than anywhere else in the UK.

The fast-flowing rivers of the Spey, Dee and Don – to name but a few – tumble down from the mountains through fertile farmland, making the waters perfect for distilling into some of the country's finest whisky and gin, flavoured with botanicals that represent the landscape.

Sea buckthorn from Dunnet Bay in the far north gives Rock Rose Gin its citrus tang, while the dried petals of the Jacobite rose add an aromatic floral quality to gins from the House of Elrick in Newmachar.

Get a taste for the region in the following pages...

The Great Scottish Gin Trail

1 ROCK ROSE
Dunnet Bay

There are two fabulous tour experiences on offer at the Dunnet Bay Distillery on the northern tip of the country. The Express Tour at £10 lasts 30 minutes and for that you get tasters of Rock Rose Gin and Holy Grass Vodka – yum! The Premium Tour at £18 lasts an hour-and-a-half and offers a much deeper delve into the distillery's processes as well as three tasters and a goody bag to take away and enjoy later – great value!
dunnetbaydistillers.co.uk

Dunnet Bay

2 THE TIPPLING HOUSE
Aberdeen

Of all the gin joints in all the world… this "subterranean late-night tavern" has to be one of the best. An inventive and delicious cocktail menu boasts a great selection of gin-based tipples, and the "grazing nibbles" menu of bar snacks like poutine or halloumi fries with chilli honey are to die for. Their gin menu changes every few months to feature the best gin from Scotland and around the world, served with flair by expert mixologists. Tasting evenings also available.
thetipplinghouse.com

3 EENOO GIN
The Lost Loch Distillery, Aboyne

This tiny distillery on the edge of the Cairngorms National Park, produces some award-winning and distinctive gin and absinthe. Take a "micro-tour" of the distillery for £25 which includes a guided tasting, talk on the history of gin, and sampling of the botanicals that make it. You also get your own branded glass to take home.
lostlochspirits.com

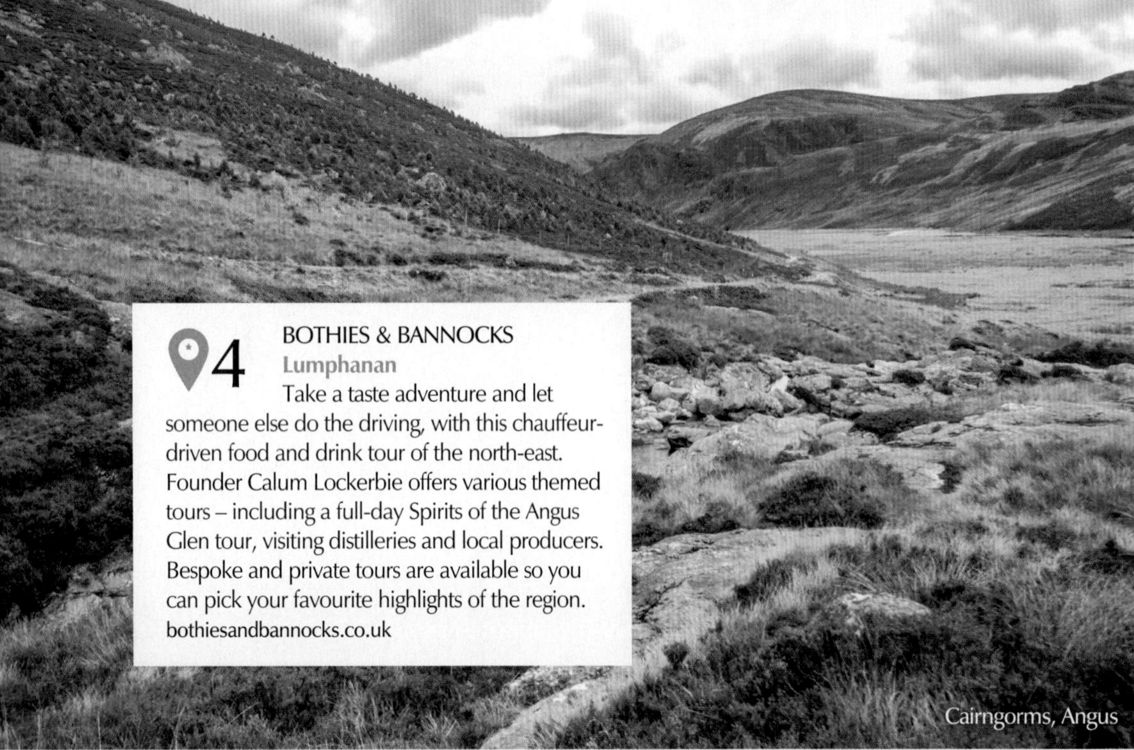
Cairngorms, Angus

4 BOTHIES & BANNOCKS
Lumphanan

Take a taste adventure and let someone else do the driving, with this chauffeur-driven food and drink tour of the north-east. Founder Calum Lockerbie offers various themed tours – including a full-day Spirits of the Angus Glen tour, visiting distilleries and local producers. Bespoke and private tours are available so you can pick your favourite highlights of the region.
bothiesandbannocks.co.uk

5 ABERDEEN DISTILLERY
Aberdeen

Join the Aberdeen Gin School and create your own gin! This three-hour experience includes a distillery tour, demonstration and classroom time – where you can pick your own botanicals and distil your perfect gin in a mini-still. Drinks are provided throughout and tickets cost £120 – great value for a top time!

cityofaberdeendistillery.co.uk

6 THE BOTHY EXPERIENCE
Glamis, Angus

Just outside the historic village of Glamis in Angus, lies the award-winning Gin Bothy distillery. The Bothy Experience is free to explore and each room is dedicated to either Scottish bothies – mountain shelters – or the history of gin. Pick up some locally-sourced food, drinks and gifts in the Bothy Larder shop, have a cup of tea and sample some home-baking in the Bothy Bakery, or settle in for a gin tasting and pairing, either with others or in your own private room.

ginbothy.co.uk

7 CAORUNN
Balmenach Distillery, Moray

Caorunn (pronounced ka-roon) is handcrafted in small batches at Balmenach Distillery in the Scottish Highlands. Pure grain spirit is infused with handpicked botanicals – six traditional and five Celtic – in the world's only working copper berry chamber. Tours of the distillery are available, with guided tasting sessions.

caorunngin.com

8 AVVA SCOTTISH GIN
Elgin

Located in the old Cathedral City of Elgin and the famous distilling region of Speyside, Avva Scottish Gin is lovingly handcrafted in Jessie-Jean, the bespoke copper still. The name Avva means a respected grandmother or elder women in the Indian language of Dravidian so it is fitting that the still is named after the distiller's two grandmothers. Pop in to visit Jessie-Jean – and Jill, the master distiller – for your microtour and sampling session.

avvascottishgin.co.uk

SPIRITS, CAORUNN GIN, CITY OF ABERDEEN DISTILLERY, THE TIPPLING HOUSE, DC THOMSON

NORTH-EAST

SEE & DO MORE

Things To Do

1 DUNNOTTAR CASTLE

Stonehaven, AB39 2TL

A few miles south of Stonehaven, lies this ruined medieval fortress, clinging to the rocks above the North Sea. The various tower houses at the castle were built between the 13th and 16th centuries, and the ruins can now be toured at your leisure. Download the free mobile map for access to an annotated map and directions, revealing the fascinating history of this remarkable site. Book your entry tickets in advance at dunnottarcastle.co.uk

2 VICTORIAN HERITAGE TRAIL

Royal Deeside

Follow a signposted route around Royal Deeside to discover both the magnificent Victorian architecture in the area and the royal residence of Balmoral Castle. Don't miss Crathie Kirkyard where many of the stones are inscribed with heartfelt messages by Queen Victoria. Find the full trail on visitscotland.com

3 ABERDEEN ART GALLERY

Aberdeen

Add a drop of culture to your trip to the north-east with a visit to Aberdeen Gallery. The collection spans more than 700 years and includes a superb range of works by artists, designers and makers. Admission is free, and the in-gallery cafe does excellent paninis.
aberdeencity.gov.uk/AAGM

4 STONEHAVEN OPEN AIR POOL

Stonehaven

This unique – and heated! – outdoor swimming pool in Stonehaven has sheltered sun terraces – perfect for adults to relax in while the kids are entertained in the paddling pool for under-eights and regular "fun sessions" with inflatables.
stonehavenopenairpool.co.uk

5 EDEN COURT THEATRE

Inverness

Scotland's largest combined arts organisation boasts two beautiful theatres, two multi-purpose studios, two cinemas and three art galleries showcasing touring art exhibitions, plays, films, concerts, comedy nights and more.
eden-court.co.uk

Pictures: KATH FLANNERY

TOP Accommodation!

Turn your gin trail into the perfect staycation...

ROYAL GOLF HOTEL

Dornoch

Expect a traditional Highland welcome in this independent hotel, just a few yards from the stunning Royal Dornoch Golf Club. The hotel offers a range of luxury suites and apartments, and a Conservatory Restaurant with unparalleled views across the golf course to the Dornoch Firth and mesmerising Dornoch Beach. Look out for dolphins while you're sampling the best of local, seasonal produce. Dogs are also welcome at an extra cost.

royalgolfhoteldornoch.co.uk

DOUNESIDE HOUSE

Aboyne

This beautiful country house near Aboyne has been tastefully converted into a luxury hotel, complete with health club and AA triple rosette-awarded restaurant. Guest rooms, apartments and even self-catering cottages in a variety of styles and sizes are available in the magnificent grounds, ensuring all groups are catered for. All are tastefully furnished in a classic-contemporary style, with antiques around every corner. It's warm, it's welcoming – it's Scottish hospitality at its finest!

dounesidehouse.co.uk

CULLEN BAY HOTEL

Cullen

Overlooking a windswept bay on the Moray coast, this contemporary hotel boasts 14 rooms and an award-winning restaurant. Guests can enjoy walks around the rugged coastline, or a game of golf right on the hotel's doorstep. Cullen is also the home of the famous Cullen skink – a hearty, full-flavoured smoked haddock soup – and Cullen Bay Hotel's restaurant has won awards for its take on the dish.

cullenbayhotel.com

THE MARCLIFFE HOTEL & SPA

Pitfodels, Aberdeen

Luxury country hotel, and once Aberdeen's first five-star hotel, set in eight acres of sumptuous gardens. The 39 rooms are furnished with Marcliffe's own signature, luxury king-size or twin mattresses with turn-down service as standard. Indulge yourself with afternoon tea in the Drawing Room and dinner in the Conservatory – choosing from an à la carte or King Crab & Lobster menu. Golf, fishing and spa packages available.

marcliffe.com

MACKAYS HOTEL

Wick

Nestled in the centre of Wick, this dog-friendly, family-run hotel welcomes guests with open arms. Choose from 30 rooms from modern to superior, or spacious holiday homes and townhouses on the doorstep. Their in-house No.1 Bistro restaurant works with local producers, such as Caithness Smokehouse, to serve guests the very best in Scottish dining, and their own Mackays Bar specialises in private tastings with the owner, accredited by the Scotch Whisky Association.

mackayshotel.co.uk

Pictures: ROYAL GOLF HOTEL, DOUNESIDE HOUSE, CULLEN BAY HOTEL, THE MARCLIFFE HOTEL & SPA, MACKAYS HOTEL

Liathach, Glen Torridon

North & West

Discover some of Scotland's most remote distilleries and stunning mountain scenery on the gin journey of a lifetime through the dramatic glens of this spectacular region

THE north and west of Scotland offer some of the country's most beautiful and dramatic scenery.

From Loch Lomond in the south to Durness in the north, you'll find a remarkable variety of glorious and ever-changing landscapes throughout the year.

The A82 takes you from Glasgow to Inverness, through Glen Coe and past some of the UK's most spectacular mountains.

For history lovers there is plenty to explore on your trail with iconic Scottish landmarks like Eilean Donan Castle to take in.

It's also geologically fascinating – as you travel farther north to Assynt and beyond you'll pass some of the oldest rock formations in the world.

The gin distilleries are fewer in number here than in other areas of Scotland, but the scenery you'll see as you journey between them make for a holiday to remember.

There is no better place to enjoy a Scottish gin than overlooking the rugged scenery of the north-west.

The Great Scottish Gin Trail

1 THE TORRIDON

Torridon

This boutique resort offers full-day activities – from clay pigeon shooting to snorkelling – a fine dining restaurant with fresh produce from their farm and kitchen garden, and before bed, some of the best gin Scotland has to offer. Their acclaimed classic-style Whisky & Gin Bar boasts 120 gins – including the resort's own Arcturus gin, distilled from fresh loch water with locally-foraged botanicals. thetorridon.com

2 PIXEL SPIRITS

North Ballachulish

This tiny craft distillery was one of the first in Scotland to begin offering full distillation courses. The Master Distiller, Craig, is on-hand to offer tours of the distillery and fascinating talks on both the gin and rum they produce. They also offer a virtual distilling experience where you direct Craig from your own home as he creates a new gin from botanicals you select. The final product is then wax-sealed and posted out to you. pixelspiritsltd.co.uk

3 RHIDORROCH DISTILLERY

Ullapool

There's an abundance of natural flavour in the lovely Loch Achall Gin, produced by the tiny Rhidorroch Distillery – within the bottle you'll find gorse flower, rowan berries, heather and a little juniper all gathered from around the loch along with the freshest water there is. While the distillery itself is too small for tours, it does have a pop-up shop in Ullapool – be sure to say hello! rhidorrochdistillery.co.uk

4 THE SEAFORTH

Ullapool

Soak up some proper Highland hospitality in this cosy bar and restaurant. It's located overlooking Ullapool's busy harbour, so you can watch the fishermen bring in the day's catch to be freshly prepared for your evening meal. Wash it down with a tipple from their excellent gin selection and get your toes tapping with regular – and occasionally impromptu – live music. theseaforth.com

5 GLEN WYVIS
Dingwall

The world's first community-owned distillery was established in 2015 after raising £2.6 million in just 77 days, and GoodWill Scottish Gin was released three years later. The gin may be relatively new but the history of distilling in Dingwall goes back to 1690. A full-bodied gin with a citrus bouquet followed by a deeper earthier finish of orris root, coriander and cinnamon.
glenwyvis.com

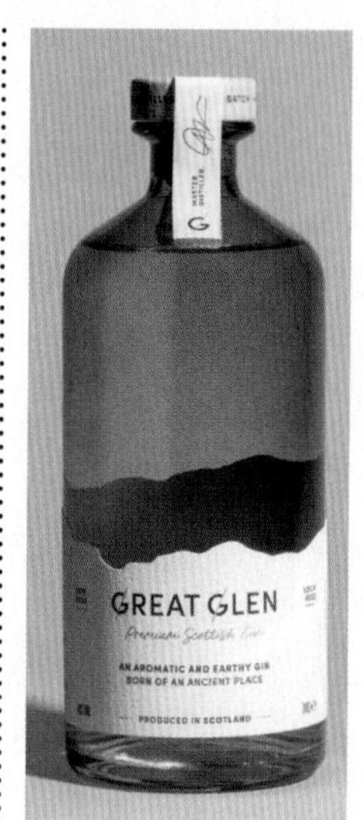

6 BEN LOMOND DISTILLING
Alexandria

The flagship gin of Ben Lomond Distilling is, as you'd imagine, Ben Lomond Scottish Gin, which is a vibrant and crisp offering from the bonnie banks – and waters – of Loch Lomond. Their infused gins, however, are where this distillery really packs its punches. Try blackberry and gooseberry gin or raspberry and elderflower for a refreshing summer taste.
lochlomondgroup.com

Loch Lomond looking on to Ben Lomond

7 GREAT GLEN DISTILLERY
Drumnadrochit

Proudly claiming itself to be Scotland's newest and smallest craft distillery, this charming little business harnesses the wildness and majesty of the Great Glen to produce its Premium Scottish Gin, made from the purest water sourced straight from Loch Ness – no chance of a monster popping up in this beautiful drink! You'll also get notes of wild Scottish heather and citrusy sheep's sorrel.
greatglendistillery.co.uk

8 DAFFY'S GIN SCHOOL
Strathmashie

Design your ultimate gin flavour profile, forage for ingredients in the hills around the distillery, then return to your personal still to distil the spirit and leave with three 20cl bottles of your signature gin! The team will lead you through the process and you will also receive a certificate. Adventurous foraging trips by 4x4 and paddleboard are also available, as is overnight accommodation in the conveniently located Distillery Cottage.
daffysgin.com

Pictures: THE TORRIDON, PIXEL SPIRITS, THE SEAFORTH, GLENWYVIS, DAFFY'S GIN

SPOTLIGHT
BADACHRO

Written In The Stars

Fate brought distillers Gordon and Vanessa together – they gave up big city life to craft gin in the Highlands

Words: EUAN DUGUID

THE coastal hamlet of Badachro is magical – nestled in the last true wilderness in the north west of Scotland, the place is teaming with fairies, demons and kelpies.

Even non-believers find themselves bewitched as the aurora borealis dance across inky skies, the belt of the Milky Way dazzling above.

Perhaps it was written in the stars that gin would be produced in this landscape where purity and botanicals abound.

And the fact that the spirit is all the by-product of a love story adds a twist to the mix.

But it took a wee while for said celestial bodies to align.

"It really is a tale of fate that brought my wife, Vanessa, and I together," says Gordon Quinn, 59, of Badachro Gin.

"Around 30 years ago I was developing a real passion for hillwalking and had always wanted to explore the Torridon mountains.

"One spring, I set off, looking forward to embracing this wilderness – but upon arriving found a wet, grey, blustery scene.

"I found shelter in the Badachro Inn. The weather actually worsened and I ended up staying the entire night, making some great new pals.

"I really fell for Badachro and kept visiting every few weeks from then on."

Vanessa, 51, takes up the tale.

"Five years on from Gordon's first visit, I was on my sixth year school trip to the Highlands from my home city of Munich.

"I fell in love with Badachro and would keep returning, but it was another five years before my path crossed with Gordon's.

"During the overlapping period Gordon and I had made friends with the same crowd and would hear each other's names mentioned, although we still hadn't met!

"One fateful weekend we both visited Badachro – and married 12 weeks later!"

Work drew Gordon, an advertising executive, and Vanessa, a horticulturist, to the Middle East where they lived for five years followed by a stint in London.

After deciding to start a family, in 2002 the pair returned to Gordon's home city of Edinburgh – but a certain hamlet beckoned.

"In 2007, we both packed in our careers, sold

BADACHRO DISTILLERY
AIRD HILL,
BADACHRO,
WESTER ROSS,
IV21 2AB

badachro
distillery.com

GORDON AND VANESSA QUINN
OWNERS

The couple's still, Delilah

our house in Edinburgh and moved to Badachro. The place had an irresistible pull on us and we've been at peace ever since."

Following a stay in a caravan, the couple – with children Sean, now 22, and Ashley, 17 – moved into their newly built home and set up their business, Aird Hill B&B and Little Aird Hill holiday cottage.

"We sold up and moved to Badachro. The place had an irresistible pull on us and we've been at peace ever since"

"Our guests would often ask, 'What souvenir should we take away from Badachro?' The local shellfish are sublime but don't tend to travel in suitcases too well!

"Vanessa – with her expertise in horticulture – and I started to consider how to make a scent from local botanicals and then, realising what was available locally, we thought we could make a liqueur. That idea morphed into a gin and Badachro Gin was born."

The local, hand-picked gorse blossom, wild myrtle and elderflower are combined with juniper berries in the couple's still, named Delilah.

From humble beginnings the product was launched in June 2017, immediately benefiting from the village's location on the North Coast 500 tourist route.

"Initially, it was just something to sell to our B&B guests," says Gordon.

"As soon as we started doing that, the Badachro Inn asked us about selling the gin.

"It's blossomed from there. From the shops around Gairloch, we're now working with distributors in the Highlands, central belt and London and export to Germany.

"We're also selling online within the UK and overseas via a partner."

Busy times – but what's it like combining married life with a business venture?

"There are pros and cons," Gordon says. "We can co-ordinate easily, discuss issues honestly and fully support each other's efforts. We're both totally invested in the business, brand and process."

Vanessa says, "The main drawback is that it's not so easy to get away together, on non-business trips. That said, we don't have much desire to leave this magical place."

Pop into the distillery in Badachro for a browse of their products, stay for a chat with the friendly team and perhaps enjoy a sample or two...

Badachro Gin

Pictures: BADACHRO

NORTH & WEST

SEE & DO MORE

Things To Do

1 SMOO CAVE

Durness

This natural, gigantic sea cave is open to the public daily and accessed via a short but steep walk from the carpark east of Durness. The cave mouth is 15 metres (50 feet) high, and a wooden bridge will take you further into the cave to see a splendid 25 metre (82 foot) waterfall. The more adventurous can book a cave tour with the resident expert that leads into the deeper and darker recesses of the natural phenomenon.

smoocavetours.com

2 THE ROCK STOP

Unapool

The North West Highlands Geopark was the first in Scotland, and protects the land from Durness to Achiltibuie. The Lewisian Gneiss rock is 3,000 million years old – the oldest in Britain. Discover how it was formed at the visitor centre in Unapool and pick up maps to exploring the area.

nwhgeopark.com

3 LANDMARK PARK

Carrbridge

Schedule a full day to take in the activities in this forest adventure park, from climbing and skydiving to mini diggers and shooting. On sunny days take the Wild Water Coaster, and if it's raining head for the Butterfly House or Bamboozeleum – packed with illusions and puzzles.

landmarkpark.co.uk

4 HIGHLAND WILDLIFE PARK

Kingussie

Discover wolves, tigers and polar bears at this safari-style park. Drive through in your car and pass bison, deer and more before walking round Monkeyfield and Wolf Wood. There are even rare animals including snow leopard cubs, born in the park in 2019.

highlandwildlifepark.org.uk

5 ICE FACTOR

Kinlochleven

Get the adrenaline pumping with indoor rock-climbing, an aerial adventure course and an indoor ice-climbing wall at this amazing activity centre. Visit the shop, and enjoy the café while you browse their extensive list of guided outdoor adventures.

ice-factor.co.uk

Pictures: THE ROCK STOP, LANDMARK, ICE FACTOR

TOP Accommodation!

Turn your gin trail into the perfect staycation...

AUCHENHEGLISH LODGES

Arden, West Dunbartonshire

For those looking for privacy as well as luxury, look no further than these self-catering cottages on the bonnie banks of Loch Lomond. The 19 cottages all have spectacular views across the loch. From cosy one-bedroom Pier Cottage to the five-bedroomed Hollybank House complete with outdoor decking and hot tub, you'll find the perfect accommodation to suit you. Guests can also access the estate's private jetty for boat trips out onto the loch.
lochlomondlodge.co.uk

INVER LODGE HOTEL

Lochinver, Assynt

The peaceful village of Lochinver sits on the North Coast 500, and this hidden gem of a hotel overlooks the head of the loch. The on-site two AA Rosette restaurant serves seasonal local produce, with all steaks, salmon and game taken from the owner's private estates. The restaurant has recently swapped its formal style of dining for a more relaxed environment – but the cuisine is still as good as ever.
inverlodge.com

STONEFIELD CASTLE

Tarbert, Argyll

Originally built in 1837 as a baronial country house, Stonefield Castle has been tastefully converted into a luxury hotel, retaining many original features. There are 38 ensuite rooms – some with four-poster beds – and a restaurant, bar, guest lounge and elegant drawing room for relaxing in. You can expect exceptional seafood in the restaurant, caught from the waters of Loch Fyne, which the hotel overlooks.
stonefieldcastlehotel.co.uk

KINGSHOUSE HOTEL

Glen Coe, Argyll

A major refurbishment and extension saw the famous Kings House, one of Scotland's oldest licensed inns, reopen with 57 rooms in 2019. Set in the Eastern end of Glen Coe and surrounded by magnificent mountains, the hotel now includes a bunkhouse for hikers, drying room, and the best of Highland hospitality. With a little help from locally sourced food, beers and spirits, you can really get away from it all here and rejuvenate.
kingshousehotel.co.uk

ATHOLL PALACE

Pitlochry, Perthshire

High above Pitlochry in Highland Perthshire, this hotel originally opened as the Athole Hydropathic, a centre for healing and restoration, in 1878. Beautifully restored and updated, the hotel still holds true to that ethos with a gym, pool, sauna and Lavender Spa offering treatments like Hot Lava Shell Massage. Accommodation includes suites, Manor House rooms, self-catering cottages, apartments and lodges in the extensive grounds.
athollpalace.com

Pictures: AUCHENHEGLISH LODGES, INVER LODGE HOTEL, STONEFIELD CASTLE, KINGSHOUSE HOTEL, ATHOLL PALACE

The Great Scottish Gin Trail

The Kelpies at Helix Park, Falkirk

Central

Taking in three of Scotland's largest cities, a tour around the heart of the country visits an array of gin distilleries alongside a host of other attractions

HOME to Edinburgh and Glasgow, Scotland's Central Belt is ideal for a gin trail.

And if you extend further north to include Dundee and Fife, you end up with a host of distilleries to choose from. You're also spoilt for things to do between tastings!

In Edinburgh, you can take in historical sights such as Holyrood Palace and the world-famous castle.

In Glasgow, enjoy some top shopping or check out the Kelvingrove Art Gallery and Museum in the West End.

The award-winning Kelpie statues at Helix Park are also conveniently located just off the M9 near Falkirk.

Make sure you have time to visit Scotland's first design museum, V&A Dundee if you're heading east, and don't forget a trip round the Kingdom of Fife to visit the postcard perfect coastal villages and the "home of golf", St Andrews.

This region also boasts some of Scotland's best gin bars, with mixologists dedicated to refining the perfect serve and inventing new gin cocktails to suit every palate...

The Great Scottish Gin Trail

1 beGIN
Byres Road, Glasgow

Do you know which garnish goes best with each individual gin – and which tonic should be served? Let the bar staff at beGIN keep you right with their extensive menu – featuring 30 different garnishes, 17 tonics and more than 100 gins from Scotland and around the world. The gins are categorised as either Scottish, classic, citrus, fruity, floral, spiced or the intriguing "weird and wonderful".
beginglasgow.com

2 CROSSBILL GIN
Barras, Glasgow

Having relocated their distillery from Aviemore to the legendary Barras in Glasgow's East End in 2017, Crossbill Distilling now have their distillery open for tours. You can take a tour to see how the first gin with 100% Scottish botanicals is created, sample some of their award-winning gin offerings in the shop and even book a masterclass in their Gin School – to have a go at distilling your own unique creation to take away.
crossbillgin.com

3 KILTY GIN
Dunblane

Distilled in the quiet cathedral city of Dunblane – childhood home of Scots tennis legend Andy Murray – Kilty Gin is made with a total of 10 carefully selected botanicals, including locally hand foraged rowan berries. The distillery is a charming family-run little venture while the gin itself is truly delicious!
kiltygin.com

4 GIN DIPLOMA
Royal Botanic Garden, Edinburgh

Edinburgh Whisky Academy has rolled out this comprehensive one-day course in Scotland's other favourite spirit – gin. Discover its history, styles and distillation in the classroom before Dr Greg Kenicer, the head botanist at the Royal Botanic Garden Edinburgh, takes you out on a botanical safari. Pre-reading material is sent out in advance and the modules are assessed – with those passing receiving an SQA-approved diploma.
edinburghwhiskyacademy.com

5 TASTE PERTHSHIRE
Perth Road, Bankfoot

A visit to Taste Perthshire, just north of Perth, will definitely leave you feeling gin-spired. Their shop boasts more than 30 gins, and you can also enjoy a tasting of their own "Hairy Coo" gin, named after the resident Highland cows. The shop and restaurant specialise in local delicacies, clothing and crafts, and stock a wide selection of gin related gifts & hampers.
tasteperthshire.co.uk/shop

6 56 NORTH
Newington, Edinburgh

This gin bar and restaurant boasts more than 350 gins on its groaning bar shelves and prides itself on being Scotland's first dedicated gin bar. The staff are happy to recommend a gin to suit every palate, and the food menu is filled with sharing platters and boards to complement your chosen tipple. Look out for their tempting cheese and gin tasting sessions, sampling the bar's own South Loch Gin – distilled on the premises.
fiftysixnorth.co.uk

7 GALLERY 48
Dundee

This stylish, bright and airy tapas bar has a formidable gin menu, served in copas de balón – gin goblets – with gourmet garnishes for a true Spanish gin bar experience. If you're feeling particularly thirsty, you can even get a 75ml Donostia measure – but it's definitely a good idea to order some of their delicious tapas plates to go with it. Their salt cod fritters and gambas al pil pil are particularly worth a nibble.
gallery48.co.uk

8 GIN CRUISE
Union Canal, Edinburgh

Lucky White Heather run a fabulous two-hour trip on the Lochrin Belle canal boat along the Union Canal starting and ending at Fountainbridge, sampling four different gins from around the country while experienced gin hosts and mixologists will discuss interesting gin topics and answer any and all questions you may have.
re-union.org.uk/gin-tasting

Pictures: CROSSBILL DISTILLERIES LTD, 56 NORTH, DARNLEY'S GIN, BEGIN, MCQUEEN GIN, EDINBURGH WHISKY ACADEMY, SUMMERHALL DRINKS LAB, DC THOMSON

A Real Slow Gin

Near Glasgow Airport, a unique gin has been quietly maturing...

Words: EUAN DUGUID

IF you snooze, you lose. Indeed, with the growth of our gin industry accelerating at bullet-train velocity in recent years, market newbies have to act fast.

Slick branding is nitro-boosted by pacey PR and, at a pragmatic level, another reason for the G-force behind gin is the relative ease of production.

Unlike whisky – which has to remain in cask for at least three years – gin can be hatched and despatched in a matter of days.

Yet, amid all this mind-spinning momentum, one sleepy spirit entered the market at a more sedate pace in 2019.

Renfrew-based independent bottlers Cumbrae Supply Company have launched a unique blend, under the trading name of House of MacDuff, which combines what's believed to be the oldest cask-aged gin in the world with a newer spirit gin.

Situated just across the White Cart Water from the high-speed bustle of Glasgow Airport, House of MacDuff present a surprisingly relaxed style.

Where most cask-conditioned gins are only in the barrel from three months to a year, the House of MacDuff's Fifty/50/Gin contains spirit that has been matured in virgin oak casks for 20 years, evoking comparisons with Rip Van Winkle.

"The idea came from our experience with single cask whisky where the flavour and colour develops during their time in the casks," says Iain MacDuff, product development manager. "At the time, we were looking for a new product to add to our portfolio and one of our suppliers offered us some London dry gin distilled at Langley Distillery.

"Because all we'd really worked with until that point was whisky, we thought it'd be interesting to cask it and see what happened. It wasn't really a conscious decision to leave it so long, but after sitting for 10 years in virgin oak barrels we realised it was becoming something interesting."

Those virgin oak casks infused sweet vanilla, ginger and oak flavours into the spirit. Since time

FIFTY/50/GIN
HOUSTON HOUSE,
95 WRIGHT STREET,
RENFREW, PA4 8AN

houseof
macduff.co.uk

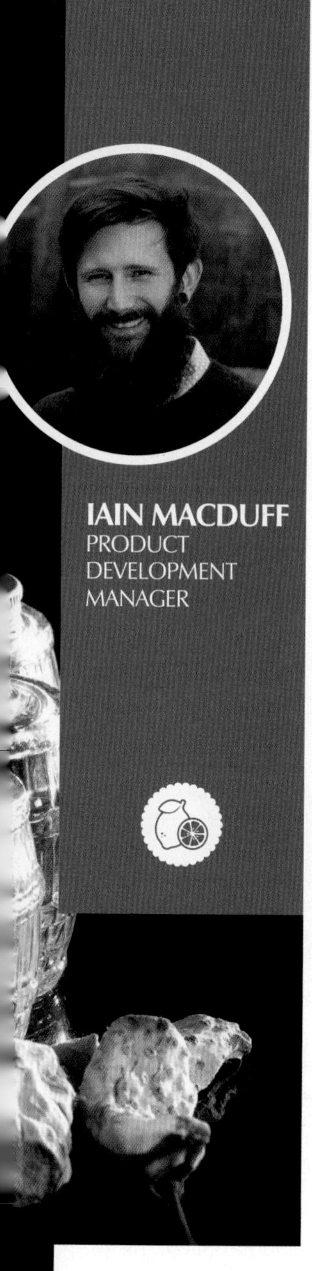

IAIN MACDUFF
PRODUCT DEVELOPMENT MANAGER

Perfect in a cocktail

plays such a great roll in maturation, for the second 10 years the House of MacDuff chose ex-whisky casks.

These allowed the wood to slowly impart greater depth and a gentle range of flavours.

"As a result of these two decades, the aged gin turned a deep golden colour," Iain says, "but it lost its juniper dominance. To bring back the juniper and complementary botanicals, we elected to combine our aged gin with new gin at a ratio of one-to-one."

And so Fifty/50 was born – as has a new understanding of how gin ages. Iain's mum Jane – the other half of this mother-and-son business – reckons that something magical has occurred in those years.

"The 20-year-old gin from the cask has flavours whisky-lovers will be familiar with," she says. "But it also has some that would never be present in whisky.

"Happily the pairing of the aged and new gin is very complimentary – with the aged gin bringing depth and body and the new gin offering a fresh brightness."

It is not the first foray into setting market firsts at the House of MacDuff.

The Cumbrae Supply Company dates back to the 1950s and became known for bottling The Smallest Bottle of Whisky in the World as listed in the *Guinness Book Of Records*.

Thereafter it was owned by the Paisley Whisky Co Ltd until 1987 when the MacDuff family purchased it.

In the 1990s, the family started to focus on bottling whisky miniatures and single casks for third parties. With a move of premises and a small bonded facility, the family began to acquire stock and bottle their own brands.

That experience – and sense of world wise calm – will set the tone for the future.

"The mainstream gin market is moving very fast," Jane says. "Maturing whisky and our gin has obviously been a slow process and we are happy to sit aside from the rush and take things at more relaxed pace.

"Unless there are other casks of gin as old as ours, no one can catch up to make something quite like Fifty/50/Gin."

What's more, the distillery now recycles their exquisite gin bottles into holders for their new natural soy wax candles. So when you really feel like a gin, but can't have one – you can light their Gin & Tonic candle for the next best thing.

"Because all we'd really worked with until that point was whisky, we thought it'd be interesting to cask it"

Jane and Iain

Pictures: HOUSE OF MACDUFF

CENTRAL
SEE & DO MORE

Things To Do

1

NATIONAL MUSEUM OF SCOTLAND

Edinburgh

Thousands of artefacts of national and international importance are on display in this giant museum. In the Science and Technology galleries you can come face-to-face with Dolly the Sheep and an evolution of aeroplanes, suspended from the ceiling. The interactive exhibits make this really popular with kids, especially the Natural World galleries, with the Tyrannosaurus Rex skeleton guarding the entrance.

nms.ac.uk

2

HELIX PARK

Falkirk

Best known as the "home of the Kelpies", Helix Park is a pet-friendly green space with paths, watersports, café – and, of course, the Kelpies. The two 30-metre (98-feet) statues commemorate both the Clydesdale horses that helped build the canal and Scotland's mythical waterhorse.

thehelix.co.uk

3

GLASGOW SCIENCE CENTRE

Glasgow

Interactive, dynamic and fun-filled, this centre is perfect for a rainy day. Young children will be entertained by science demos and optical illusions, while older kids enjoy the Space Zone, and adults relax in the café.

glasgowsciencecentre.org

4

DISCOVERY POINT

Dundee

Award-winning attraction telling the story of the *RSS Discovery* ship, the last traditional wooden three-masted ship built in the UK. *Discovery* survived being stuck in the Antarctic ice for two years on Captain Scott's 1901 expedition.

rrsdiscovery.co.uk

5

STIRLING CASTLE

Stirling

One of the largest and most important in Scotland, the castle has had a commanding presence over the area since the 12th century. Scottish kings and queens were crowned here, including Mary, Queen of Scots, who spent her early years in the castle.

stirlingcastle.scot

TOP Accommodation!

Turn your gin trail into the perfect staycation...

CRIEFF HYDRO

Crieff, Perthshire

Set in its own 365-hectare (900-acre) estate this legendary resort is hard to beat for fantastic scenery and luxury. First-class facilities abound with golf, tennis, leisure and fitness studios, and even an adventure park for kids. A range of rooms, suites and separate self-catering lodge accommodation is available, while six on-site restaurants and cafés offers guests a great variety of choice. When booking directly, each hotel guest is eligible for a complementary Scottish breakfast.

crieffhydro.com

THE PEAT INN

St Andrews, Fife

What may seem like a modest small hotel and restaurant in rural Fife is in fact one of Scotland's most sensational hidden gems. Nestled between St Andrews and Cupar, this sublime Michelin-starred restaurant also boasts eight luxury suites. Lose yourself in wonderful Scottish dishes, whether you choose the four-course chef's menu at lunch, including sea bream and wood pigeon, or the dinner menu with Islay oysters.

thepeatinn.co.uk

RADISSON RED

Glasgow

At the heart of Glasgow's Finnieston Quay, this modern four-star hotel is a stone's throw from the Scottish Event Campus. Opened in 2018, the hotel is well known as the home of the popular Red Sky Bar. Glasgow's first rooftop bar takes you to the top of the eight-floor hotel where locally-inspired cocktails await. The panoramic city views are the real cherry on top.

radissonhotels.com/en-us/hotels/radisson-red-glasgow

CROMLIX HOTEL

Kinbuck, Dunblane

Situated near Dunblane, this Victorian mansion house was re-opened as a luxury hotel in 2014 under new owner, tennis star Sir Andy Murray. Settled within 34 acres of woodland, Cromlix has 10 rooms and five suites, all of which are individually designed with grandeur and comfort in mind. The Glasshouse is a place to relax and enjoy fine food and exquisite afternoon tea. The hotel also offers activities including fishing and, of course, tennis.

cromlix.com

SHERATON GRAND

Edinburgh

Prepare to be pampered in this five-star spa hotel, right in the centre of Edinburgh. Luxury rooms and suites have unparalleled views of the castle. The Sheraton Grand's spa facilities are the perfect place to relax, with a whole range of experiences and treatments on offer. Chill in the Himalayan dry salt room, marvel at Edinburgh's skyline in the rooftop hydropool or enjoy a soothing couple's massage.

marriott.com/hotels/travel/edisi-sheraton-grand-hotel-and-spa-edinburgh

Pictures: CRIEFF HYDRO, THE PEAT INN, RADISSON RED, CROMLIX HOTEL, SHERATON GRAND

Scott's View looking to the Eildon Hills and the River Tweed

South

The south of Scotland is home to verdant, rolling scenery as well as plenty of historical and cultural spots to visit between distilleries

SECLUDED craft distilleries lie in wait, nestled in the rolling hills of the Borders and Dumfries and Galloway.

With beautiful hills and scenic lochs in the west giving way to pretty fishing villages like St Abbs in the east, there's plenty of scenery to appreciate between your gin tastings.

Visit the historical and picturesque towns of Kelso, Jedburgh, Dryburgh and Melrose to visit the four beautiful Borders Abbeys and take in some history.

Pop into the magnificent Floors Castle for a taste of history or head to Scotland's Book Town, Wigtown, to lose yourself in one of their 14 fantastic bookshops.

The gins of Scotland's south are steeped in local legend, taking inspiration from old Borders tales and local botanicals.

Whether you are looking for a scenic or historical walking trail, a beachside getaway or a spot of arts, crafts and culture then head to southernmost Scotland for a gin trail you'll never forget.

The Great Scottish Gin Trail

1 INSPIRITED GIN
Strathaven

Known for its innovative and fun approach to gin distilling, Inspirited allows customers to create their own unique gin by selecting from a wide range of botanicals. Produced in small batches, each bottle is crafted to high-quality standards, ensuring a distinct and personalised flavour profile. Inspirited Gin appeals to adventurous gin enthusiasts seeking a memorable drinking experience, combining tradition with modern creativity. inspirited.co.uk

2 BRODIES
Moffat

This restaurant, gin and coffee lounge opened in 2016, as the first of its kind in Dumfries and Galloway. The owners are proud to showcase local gins and even have their own gin club. Private tastings can be booked, or simply relax with an afternoon tea – with a gin twist, of course. brodiesofmoffat.co.uk

3 SOLWAY SPIRITS
Annan

Distiller couple Andrew and Kate distil, bottle and label all their spirits by hand in a labour of love. Their micro-distillery only produces 50 bottles of spirit per batch – but they produce 15 different gins and flavoured gins, plus three rums and a vodka or two. Visit their new shop in Annan to meet the team and sample their varied spirit collection. solwayspirits.co.uk

4 THE WEE FARM DISTILLERY
Forth, South Lanarkshire

Be sure to visit this charming producer which is an extension of a family-run, working farm. Its unique integration of farming and distilling allows it to combine local ingredients with sustainable practices and its flagship Drovers Gin is a testament to this philosophy. theweefarmdistillery.co.uk

5 GALLOWAY GIN ESCAPE

Crafty Distillery, Newton Stewart

Tour the unspoilt hills and coastlines of Galloway as you help the makers of Hills & Harbour Gin forage for botanicals, including bladderwrack seaweed and noble fir. On your return to the distillery, you'll be taught how to turn them into delicious gin cocktails to accompany you on your tour of the distillery. Would you expect anything less from the Scottish Gin Distillery of the Year 2020? craftydistillery.com

6 KERR'S GIN

The Borders Distillery, Hawick

Local barley is used to produce single malt whisky, Kerr's Gin and Puffing Billy Steam Vodka in this former Edwardian electrical works, given a five-star rating by VisitScotland. Take a tour to discover how all three spirits are created – with generous samples along the way. thebordersdistillery.com

7 PENTLAND HILLS GIN

West Linton

Pentland Hills Gin is a premium, handcrafted gin produced in the scenic hills of its title. Known for its distinct blend of botanicals, this small-batch gin captures the essence of the Scottish landscape. Key ingredients include juniper, coriander, and lemon peel, along with unique local ingredients such as heather and Scots pine needles. The gin has smooth, crisp taste and aromatic complexity, and offers a true taste of Scotland. pentlandhillsgin.com

8 1881 DISTILLERY & GIN SCHOOL

Peebles Hydro, Peebles

A "spring to spirit" distillery, 1881 takes water straight from their private spring Shieldgreen, and turns it into four premium and unique gins, Hydro Gin, Pavilion Gin, Honours Gin and Rafters Gin. Their gin school is the largest residential one in the UK, offering a range of gin distillery tours and distiller experiences – before staying the night in the spa hotel. Explore the gardens of Peebles Hydro, meet Felicity the gleaming copper still, and craft your own gin to your heart's content. 1881distillery.com

Pictures: CRAFTY DISTILLERY, THE BORDER DISTILLERY, WEE FARM DISTILLERY, 1881 DISTILLERY, SOLWAY SPIRITS, BRODIES OF MOFFAT

Rich Flavour

This unique fruit cake gin turns a humble Selkirk bannock into a tantalising elixir

Words: EUAN DUGUID

THE humble bannock – think flat, quick bread – is a Scottish staple. Like the wonderful variance of Scottish dialect, however, the Selkirk bannock of the Borders is very different to bannocks from other parts of Scotland.

Down here, it's a rich and buttery leavened tea bread. A big contrast to the sweet and nutty bere bannocks you find up in Orkney, for instance.

And following centuries of tradition, it's still made by many local bakeries who pride themselves on a slow fermentation of the dough – lending to that deep richness.

It's not just food. This is an energy-giving source, woven into the life-rhythm of this textile-famed town.

It's perhaps little wonder, then, the bannock has not only provided the inspiration for a new local gin, but is one of the main ingredients in the distillation.

"Bannock Gin is a 'fruit cake' gin that uses Selkirk Gin as its base," says Allan Walker, CEO of Selkirk Distillers.

"The traditional fruit cake is added to our Selkirk Gin and allowed to macerate for approximately 12 weeks. The rich, buttery flavour and colours are thus released – creating a 'bannock in a bottle!'"

Allan says Bannock Gin is best served straight over ice, and treated as an after-dinner spirit to slowly sip on.

"Alternatively, the spicy, fruitiness of its flavours can be accentuated by adding ginger ale and a squeeze of lime over ice.

"It's a tantalising elixir where sweet meets savoury."

It's also reflective of the confluence of human experience that's given life to Selkirk Distillers itself.

"I'm a retired police officer," says Allan. "I left the force more than a decade ago to launch a social enterprise, Build Rwanda, dedicated to help build a school in Rwanda.

"Social enterprise is really about finding solutions, building connections and making things happen.

"I have an entrepreneurial streak, too, and in my spare time I enjoyed working with many craft food and drink businesses to help them grow."

A traditional Selkirk bannock

BANNOCK GIN
SELKIRK DISTILLERY,
THE OLD JOINERY,
PHILIPHAUGH ESTATE,
SELKIRK, TD7 5LU

t:01750 725300
selkirkdistillers.com

ALLAN WALKER
CEO
SELKIRK DISTILLERS

"The spicy, fruitiness of its flavours can be accentuated by adding ginger ale and a squeeze of lime over ice"

Selkirk in the Scottish Borders

1953 Gin and Selkirk Gin

This led to a friendship with renowned craft distiller and founder of Strathearn Distillery, Tony Reeman-Clark.

Their partnership saw the birth of Selkirk Distillers in 2017 as the duo looked to put the Scottish Borders firmly on the gin map.

But they say behind every great man there's a great woman, and this is certainly true in the case of Selkirk Distillers.

"I actually met my wife Jane when I was selling stock, including gin, at Scott's Selkirk, an annual local festival," Allan says.

"It was our love of quality gin brought that brought us together in the first place.

"It was important to Jane that the distillery, and the spirits that were created there, would foster the historical and cultural significance of Selkirk in particular, and the Scottish Borders as a whole."

Jane was diagnosed with MS 10 years ago, and the support she has received from the MS Society has made her determined to fundraise for the charity, founded in 1953.

Selkirk's latest offering, the 1953 Gin, is a fresh, fragrant, floral spirit – and the sale of each bottle contributes £10 to the society.

The distillery is based in the Old Joinery on the Philiphaugh Estate, owned by Sir Michael Strang Steel. The estate's walled gardens provide ingredients for seasonal liqueurs, which the distillery also produces.

Handpicked fruits and herbs have been used in small batches of White Currant & Mint, Sloe Berry & Spiced Apple, Plum and Bramble liqueurs.

Natural resources abound here, but the gins are also inspired by the local culture.

The town's name means "kirk of the forest". Bonnie Prince Charlie, the Marquis of Montrose and the Outlaw Murray all had strong connections here.

The bannocks are part of this heady historical broth which this fledging operation is distilling down nicely.

This brilliant distillery will be another compelling feature of the town long into the future.

Pictures: SHUTTERSTOCK, ALAMY, ROB GRAY PHOTOGRAPHS, SELKIRK DISTILLERS

THE SOUTH

SEE & DO MORE

Things To Do

1

ABBOTSFORD HOUSE

Melrose

The beloved home of 19th-century author Sir Walter Scott, Abbotsford is the perfect place to visit for anyone interested in Scott's life. You can tour the study and see the very desk where Scott wrote his most famous works of literature. Browse his personal library too for an insight into what inspired this famous novelist, and see the correspondence with other literary greats that Scott left behind. The garden, designed by Scott with advice from architects, is a rare example of a Regency layout.

scottsabbotsford.com

2

DUMFRIES & GALLOWAY AVIATION MUSEUM

Dumfries

Located at the old watchtower of RAF Dumfries, this independent museum has a vast collection of aircraft and artefacts. You'll find restored planes, including the Loch Doon Spitfire, which fought in the Battle of Britain and was recovered from Loch Doon in the 1970s.

dumfriesaviationmuseum.com

4

DRUMLANRIG CASTLE

Thornhill

On the Queensberry Estate, this A-listed castle holds more than meets the eye. Tours are offered of the castle itself, while self-catering accommodation is available in the 90,000 acre estate. Fishing and cycling are popular activities here and the adventure playground will keep little ones entertained.

drumlanrigcastle.co.uk

3

EASTGATE THEATRE & ARTS CENTRE

Peebles

The biggest and busiest arts centre of its type in the Borders, Eastgate has a cinema, theatre and workshop for creative classes. Festivals take place at the venue so keep an eye on their website. A café bar offers light bites and stronger sips.

eastgatearts.com

5

CALEDONIA PARK DESIGNER OUTLET

Gretna

If a spot of shopping is what your trip needs, then look no further. This outdoor outlet has big brand stores at bargain prices, from Levi's to Cadbury, Trespass to Le Creuset. There are also cafés and restaurants, if all that shopping makes you a little peckish.

caledoniapark.com

TOP Accommodation!

Turn your gin trail into the perfect staycation...

THE PORTPATRICK HOTEL

Portpatrick

This luxurious hotel boasts some unrivalled views across the charming seaside village of Portpatrick and the rugged Galloway coastline. The hotel itself is ideal for families, couples and solo travellers alike with comfortable rooms and a warm welcome guaranteed. The area is a haven for sports lovers and outdoor types, with a wide range of activities available nearby – such as golf at the nearby Dunskey Golf Club, birdwatching, walking and fishing.

portpatrickhotel.co.uk

ROULOTTE RETREAT

Bowden, near Melrose

Looking for something a little different? These roulotte caravans – think traditional, wooden Romany caravans with electricity and eco hot tubs – offer a rustic escape, overlooking a lochan in the Scottish Borders. Each has a double bedroom, shower and toilet, plus relaxing area and balcony. The roulottes are adult-only, but they offer a cottage for families and pets. Don't worry – it comes with its own roulotte, too.

roulotteretreat.com

KNOCKINAAM LODGE

Near Portpatrick

Once a Victorian hunting lodge, this a hotel to retreat to when you want to get away from it all, go for walks on the beach, relax in warm and comfortable surroundings and savour outstanding Scottish food. Foodies will love the seven-course tasting menu, the morning tea trays and the homemade shortbread. The hotel boasts incredible attention to detail with unrivalled service.

knockinaamlodge.com

TRAQUAIR HOUSE

Innerleithen

Spend the night in royal luxury in Scotland's oldest inhabited house. The country pile has been visited by 27 Scottish kings and queens since building began in 1107, and boasts extensive grounds, a maze and even a brewery on-site. Four exclusive and spacious rooms are available for B&B, with a house in the grounds open for self-catered stays. Don't miss the events held at the house, including the Beyond Borders International Festival.

traquair.co.uk

BLACKADDIE COUNTRY HOUSE HOTEL

Sanquhar

Owned by experienced chef Ian McAndrew – who won his first Michelin Star aged just 27 – and his wife Jane, you can be assured of a warm welcome at the family-owned Blackaddie Country House Hotel. Blackaddie is all about fabulous food, friendly service and making guests feel at home. The warm, relaxed atmosphere, luxurious rooms and delicious food make Blackaddie the perfect place for a romantic break or a relaxing weekend away.

blackaddiehotel.co.uk

Pictures: THE PORTPATRICK HOTEL, ROULOTTE RETREAT, KNOCKINAAM LODGE, TRAQUAIR HOUSE, BLACKADDIE COUNTRY HOUSE HOTEL

White sandy beach
near the Strand, Colonsay

Islands

The Scottish isles are the jewels in the country's crown, and the gins they produce are as distinctive as the islands themselves

A TOUR of Scotland's islands is fantastic at the best of times, and when you add gin to the mix you have the perfect Scottish getaway.

Beginning in the north with Shetland and Orkney, you'll find a gateway to Scotland's ancient past.

Visit the neolithic settlement of Skara Brae, Mousa Iron Age broch, and Maes Howe chambered cairn. The Inner and Outer Hebrides off Scotland's west coast have so much to offer, and their seafood and beaches are second to none.

On Skye, make the most of the fantastic restaurants serving local delicacies, providing the perfect foodie addition to your gin trail.

On Harris and Lewis, take in the glorious beaches that seem more akin to the Caribbean than the shores of Scotland.

You'll find a gin distillery on all of the country's main islands. Each uses local botanicals and each spirit is inspired by the island's heritage and natural landscape, making them the perfect starting point for a spot of island hopping.

1 GIN LOVERS RETREAT

Wild Thyme, Colonsay

This ultimate relaxing gin holiday includes two nights' dinner, bed and breakfast, picnic-style lunches, gin cocktails, a five-gin tasting – and, of course, a selection of more than 200 gins to try at your leisure. With the remote Hebridean beauty of tiny Colonsay surrounding you, this is the perfect place to unwind among untouched beaches and rugged cliffs, and sample Scotland's top spirits.
wildthymespirits.com

2 THE BOTANIST COCKTAIL CLASSES

The Botanist, Islay

Bruichladdich Distillery is one of the biggest exports of Islay whisky, and in 2001 released their first gin, The Botanist. Featuring 22 hand-foraged botanicals from Islay, this gin celebrates island life and getting back to nature. On a distillery tour you can learn all about their Islay dry gin, visit the gin still – named Ugly Betty – and learn how to make delicious gin cocktails, with a sample or two for inspiration.
thebotanist.com

3 WOMEN IN GIN

Isle of Cumbrae

The gins of Isle of Cumbrae Distillers celebrate the isle itself – from Croc Rock, named after Millport's Crocodile Rock to their award-winning main staple Nostalgin, harking back to holidays on the isle in the '50s. The distillery is run by one of the few all-female distilling teams in Scotland, and a tour of their distillery includes an engaging talk on the role of women in gin's history.
isleofcumbrae-distillers.com

Portree, Skye

4 ISLE OF SKYE GIN SCHOOL

Portree, Skye

Get hands-on with the producers of Misty Isle gin and Tommy's Gin – the Isle of Skye Distillers. Learn the history of distilling on the island at the shop in Portree, before the essential gin tasting – plus refreshments – and the opportunity to distil your own Skye spirit in your own individual copper pot still.
isleofskyedistillers.com

5 WHISKY GIN & CHOCOLATE TOUR

Raasay

The Isle of Raasay Hebridean Distillers have a tour with a difference in their small craft distillery. Visitors can enjoy a guided tasting featuring their single malt and gin, expertly paired with handmade chocolates from the Glenshiel Chocolate Company. Don't miss the chance to taste the specially commissioned Isle of Raasay single malt-infused chocolate.
raasaydistillery.com

6 SHETLAND REEL

Unst, Shetland

Saxa Vord Distillery is the most northerly distillery in the UK, and closer to Norway than it is to mainland Scotland. The trip to Shetland is more than worth your while, however, as the brains behind Shetland Reel gin have turned a former RAF site on Unst into an award-winning tourist resort with year-round self-catering accommodation, seasonal hostel, bar and restaurant – and the distillery itself.
shetlandreel.com

7 KIRKJUVAGR GIN-MAKING EXPERIENCE

Kirkwall, Orkney

Kirkjuvagr Gin is inspired by Orkney's Viking heritage, and its botanical list includes Angelica, brought to the island by Vikings thousands of years ago. Mix this with your choice of botanicals to distil your own spirit in the Orkney Gin School, or opt for a classic tour and tasting. The distillery is also child-friendly, with goody bags, and non-alcoholic options at tastings.
orkneydistilling.com

8 COMMUNITY SPIRIT

Isle of Harris Distillery

Go behind the scenes to discovery the beating heart of Harris, the Isle of Harris Distillery. From its community-driven beginnings and funding to its social projects designed to give back to its Outer Hebridean home, you can discover the story of Harris gin on a tour of its state-of-the-art distillery. Don't miss the chance to enjoy other world-famous Harris exports from Harris Tweed in the distillery shop to seafood pairings in the canteen.
harrisdistillery.com

Pictures: WILD THYME SPIRITS, RAASAY DISTILLERY, ISLE OF HARRIS DISTILLERY, THE BOTANIST, ISLE OF CUMBRAE DISTILLERS, ORKNEY DISTILLING

View to Berneray, North Uist

An Island Elixir

New gin on the block Downpour is the first one made on Scotland's outermost Hebridean isle, North Uist

Words: EUAN DUGUID

IT'S long been established that the perfect tonic to a scorching summer's day is the well-named gin and tonic. And what better elixir to cool you down than a healthy measure of new gin on the block, Downpour?

The first gin to be made on Scotland's outermost Hebridean island of North Uist, you'd be forgiven for thinking it was named after the unmitigated brunt of the Atlantic.

"No, it's named after the flavour cloud – the pearly white haze that you get in some gins when it's mixed with tonic and ice," says Jonny Ingledew, Downpour's windswept and interesting master distiller.

"Basically, it's a flavour downpour.

"It's the result of tasty essential oils coming out of solution from the alcohol concentration and temperature dropping.

"It's also referred to as louching, but we think flavour cloud better portrays this lovely rarity, as it indicates that the gin is big on the taste buds."

Sounds dreamlike – and in many ways it is. Creative director Kate MacDonald runs North Uist Distillery Co. alongside Jonny.

The entrepreneurial couple are both North Uist natives who returned to the island with the dream

DOWNPOUR GIN
NORTH UIST DISTILLERY CO.

of creating outstanding artisan spirits, after trying out a variety of careers.

"We both grew up in North Uist and left to go to university," says Kate.

"Jonny did his first degree at Edinburgh University, in physical geography and geology. He then returned to Uist to work on his dad's lobster and prawn fishing boat.

"After that he retrained and gained a masters in oil and gas engineering before working in the industry for seven years.

"I studied painting at the Edinburgh College of Art," says Kate, "before training and working as a florist.

"After being involved in many arts education projects I went on to do a post grad in art and design for secondary teaching at Strathclyde University."

However, the lure of their island home proved strong – as did the increasing feasibility of their long-held dream.

"We always knew we wanted to move back to Uist. We wanted to create our own jobs and set up a business that would have a long-term positive impact in Uist.

"The distillery was definitely something we

NORTH UIST DISTILLERY CO.
NORTH UIST,
OUTER HEBRIDES

t: 07763 854022
northuistdistillery.com

Wildflowers in the machair, North Uist

planned long before we made the move – Jonny retrained in the industry, studying brewing and distilling at Heriot-Watt University after his stint in oil and gas."

On North Uist, the couple hand-pick heather and flowers for their gin, harvesting in later summer – skills learned on the mainland.

"Kate is a trained florist and has a passion for traditional uses of flora, so along with professional forager Mark Williams, of Galloway Wild Foods, she was able to identify plants we could use," says Jonny.

"We both grew up on Uist – it's important to us that our gin is distilled, bottled and labelled on the island"

Kate and Jonny

Kate says, "Jonny was involved with a lot of project management when he worked in the oil industry, so he looked after the project budget, timeline and ordering equipment for our gin distillery.

"He's also very hands-on in the planning application phase of the whisky distillery that we are currently fundraising for."

The focus, for the time being, is on gin. In the small batch distillery, each run of the still produces 100 bottles of Downpour. There is a double run each day to build up stock, then a few days are spent bottling it.

"We're just about keeping up with demand at the moment," says Kate. "We sold 1,500 bottles in our first month of trading, primarily through our website.

"Our next step is to reach out and get Downpour stocked more widely, so people can try our full-flavoured gin!"

As sales grow, there's a healthy glow on North Uist – an island faced, in recent times, with the troubling and wider spectre of depopulation and the loss of young folk.

"There's a recent resurgence in young people moving to Uist. The distillery is just one of many start-up businesses.

"We both grew up on Uist, so it's important to us that each bottle is distilled, bottled and labelled on the island to enable the business to have a long-term benefit for people here," Kate says.

"We have been overwhelmed by the encouragement and support we've been shown and Uist will be at the heart of all of our decision-making as we develop the distillery."

Since their first gin offering, North Uist Distillery Co. has created a range of flavoured gins – including Pink Grapefruit and Sloe & Bramble.

Kate and Jonny have also released their new Oak-Aged Negroni, while they wait for their whisky to mature.

Downpour might be reminiscent of a classic Scottish deluge, but North Uist Distillery Co. has a bright outlook ahead.

Pictures: NORTH UIST DISTILLERY, CARA FORBES

ISLANDS
SEE & DO MORE

Things To Do

1 LUSKENTYRE SANDS

Harris

Consistently voted one of the world's best beaches, a trip to the Isle of Harris isn't complete without a visit to Luskentyre. Located on the west coast of South Harris, the white sand stretches for miles, offering spectacular views over the turquoise water. The sand dunes and views to the island of Taransay and the surrounding hills create a unique and magnificent setting. There's no better place to find peace, relax and spend a beautiful day.

2 DUNVEGAN CASTLE & GARDENS

Skye

The home of Clan MacLeod for 800 years, and the oldest continually inhabited castle in Scotland, Dunvegan Castle has plenty to offer. Sitting on Loch Dunvegan, the views are unrivalled, and their tours are packed with history.

dunvegancastle.com

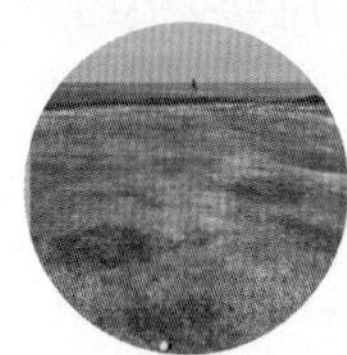

3 ASKERNISH GOLF CLUB

South Uist

Grab your clubs and get ready for a round at the oldest golf club on the Western Isles, founded on the dunes of Askernish Farm in 1891. Askernish is a unique golf course on the South Uist coast, one of the many amazing courses in Scotland.

askernishgolfclub.com

4 SKARA BRAE PREHISTORIC VILLAGE

Orkney

A UNESCO World Heritage site and Western Europe's best-preserved Neolithic village, Skara Brae paints a captivating picture of life 5,000 years ago with ancient jewellery and tools on display.

historicenvironment.scot/visit-a-place/places/skara-brae

5 SHETLAND MUSEUM & ARCHIVES

Shetland

An award-winning museum, there's plenty to see here. With a vast collection relating to Shetland, the museum is the best place to learn more about the archipelago. Events and exhibitions are updated regularly so no visit is the same as the last.

shetlandmuseumandarchives.org.uk

Pictures: ASKERNISH GOLF CLUB

THE COTTAGE STEIN

Stein, Isle of Skye

Situated in the conservation village of Stein on the stunning Waternish peninsula, this bed and breakfast has been lovingly created to provide stylish accommodation, while retaining the warmth and character of a traditional Skye cottage. The superb location offers uninterrupted sea views, with the additional bonus of being within two minutes' walking distance of the popular Stein Inn – the oldest inn on the island – and the Michelin-starred Loch Bay Restaurant.

thecottagestein.co.uk

THE HOUSE OVER-BY

Colbost, Isle of Skye

Part of the famous Three Chimneys restaurant, the House Over-By is a comfy place to stay, especially for foodies looking for a delicious meal. The restaurant serves up the very best of Scottish ingredients with the freshest produce. Each of the six beautifully appointed rooms are perfect for a romantic retreat, an escape from the city or to celebrate a special occasion on the shores of Loch Dunvegan.

threechimneys.co.uk/rooms

ISLE OF MULL HOTEL AND SPA

Craignure, Isle of Mull

This newly-renovated four-star Mull hotel boasts luxury bedrooms alongside the beautiful Driftwood Spa. Offering revitalising treatments, thermal experiences and a sea view swimming pool, the spa is the perfect place to relax after a day exploring Mull. Local produce is showcased at their bistro, Òran na Mara, with a menu inspired by seafood from the waters around Mull.

crerarhotels.com/isle-of-mull-hotel-spa

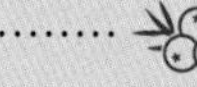

THE MACHRIE HOTEL

Islay

Set in the dunes of Islay, The Machrie Hotel and Golf Links enjoys an enviable location, nestled beside the 11km (seven-mile) Machrie beach in the Inner Hebrides. Opened in late summer 2018 after a complete renovation and expansion, The Machrie Hotel features 47 beautifully designed rooms, suites and lodges. The Machrie is focused on luxury – with their comfortable rooms, decadent restaurant and tranquil spa, it is the perfect retreat for rest and relaxation. Every one of your daily troubles will disappear here.

campbellgrayhotels.com/machrie

STROMNESS HOTEL

Stromness, Orkney

Located conveniently near the Northlink ferry terminal in Stromness, this grand hotel and restaurant has been welcoming visitors since 1901. The bay windows of the lounge bar overlook the picturesque harbour of the historic seaport and Scapa Flow. Enjoy the finest local Orcadian produce from the hotel's a la carte menu in the restaurant, or sip a gin in the quiet Victorian garden or lively Flattie Bar before retiring to one of 42 ensuite rooms.

stromnesshotel.com

Pictures: THE COTTAGESTEIN, THE HOUSE OVER-BY, ISLE OF MULL HOTEL AND SPA, THE MACHRIE HOTEL, PORT CHARLOTTE HOTEL

WOULD YOU Believe It?

Drink in these fascinating facts about gin!

During the Prohibition Era in America, homemade gin was often produced in small batches in bathtubs, giving rise to the term "bathtub gin".

★ Old Tom Gin, a sweeter style of gin, was popular in 18th-century England and is experiencing a resurgence in modern craft cocktails.

★ Genever, a Dutch precursor to modern gin, is made from malt wine and botanicals and has a distinctively malty flavour.

★ In Spain, the Gin and Tonic is not just a cocktail but an art form. Bars often offer extensive G&T menus with various brands and garnishes.

★ Some people believe that soaking raisins in gin and then eating them can help alleviate the symptoms of arthritis, although there's little scientific evidence to support this claim.

In the early 20th century, Russians also used gin as a remedy for arthritis by rubbing it on their joints and then wrapping them in bear skins.

During the Jazz Age in the 1920s, gin was the preferred spirit of choice among flappers and jazz enthusiasts, leading to the popularity of cocktails like the Gin Rickey and the Bee's Knees.

★ During the British colonial era in India, quinine, a key ingredient in tonic water, was used to prevent malaria. The addition of gin made the bitter tonic more palatable, leading to the creation of the G&T.

★ Some historic gin palaces in London, such as The Viaduct Tavern, are rumoured to be haunted. It's said that the spirits of Victorian gin drinkers still linger.

★ In 2015, a company called Cambridge Distillery sent a vial of gin into space to create the world's first cosmic gin. The gin was infused with botanicals that were exposed to low gravity aboard a weather balloon.

The extravagant decorations and furnishings of Victorian gin palaces were not just opulent but also dangerous. Many palaces were destroyed in fires due to the combination of flammable decor and open flames from gas lighting.

★ Sloe gin is made by infusing gin with sloe berries, a type of wild plum.

★ London dry gin doesn't have to be made in London. It's a style of gin characterised by its dryness and balance of botanical flavours.

★ Gin has a strong historical connection with the Jewish community. During the Inquisition, Sephardic Jews brought the art of distillation to Europe and played a significant role in the development of gin in England and the Netherlands.

★ The term "Dutch courage" originated from the English soldiers in the Thirty Years' War who drank gin for bravery before battle.

★ The most expensive bottle of gin ever sold was a bottle of Morus LXIV, priced at £4,000. It was infused with leaves from the oldest Mulberry tree in Britain.

★ The famous quote, "I never drink anything stronger than gin before breakfast" is attributed to British writer W.C. Fields.

★ In the 19th century, gin was often sold in ceramic jars known as "gin pigs" which could be refilled at local pubs.

The aroma of juniper, the primary botanical in gin, is similar to the smell of pine trees. In fact, early distillers used to add juniper to mask impurities in their spirits, which eventually led to the development of gin as we know it today.

Recipe: KATHRYN HAWKINS
Picture: STUART MACGREGOR

Half BAKED

Have your cake and eat it with this zesty gin-infused triumph

INGREDIENTS

- **225g caster sugar**
- **2 medium eggs**
- **4 tbsp whole milk**
- **150g baking margarine**
- **225g self-raising flour**
- **10 juniper berries, finely chopped**
- **8 tbsp gin**
- **110ml tonic water**
- **200g icing sugar**
- **Lemon and lime slices to decorate (jelly slices are also good!)**

METHOD

1 Preheat the oven to 190°C/Gas Mark 5. Grease and line a 20x30cm cake tin.

2 Put 150g caster sugar in a mixing bowl with the eggs, milk, margarine, flour and juniper berries. Whisk together until well blended.

3 Spoon the mixture into the tin, smooth the top and bake for 30 minutes until golden and firm to the touch.

4 Meanwhile, put the gin and 75ml tonic water in a saucepan with the remaining sugar. Heat gently, stirring until the sugar dissolves. Raise the heat and boil for 4-5 minutes until lightly syrupy.

5 Once the cake is baked, skewer the top several times. Spoon the gin and tonic mixture over the skewered cake and leave to cool in the tin.

6 Cut into 16 pieces. Sift the icing sugar into a bowl and blend with enough tonic water to make a smooth icing. Spread thickly over the cake pieces and leave to set for a few minutes. Decorate with lemon and lime slices and then devour.

The 5 Most LEGENDARY Parties Of All Time

And you thought your Aunty Mabel was wild after a couple of gins…

SULTAN Of Swing

The Sultan of Brunei does not mess around when it comes to celebrating his birthday. When Sultan Haji Hassanal Bolkiah turned 50, money was no object. To throw a party for the ages he had a brand-new stadium built just to hold a concert in his honour. Guests were treated to the finest champagne and caviar, and no-one went home without their very own gold medal. To top it all off, the Sultan hired Michael Jackson to perform for his guests – but didn't even watch the show himself.

HORSING Around

Partying isn't all gin and juice: some people prefer a classier affair. 19th Century Industrialist, CKG Billings, was one of those people. He wanted to hold a dinner at his new private stable, but when reporters found out he had to change venue. He hoofed it to a ballroom in New York, covering the ground in turf and filling the room with plants. He and his guests then dressed in suits and dined on horseback – the horses even carried Champagne in their saddle bags. Obviously.

Words: WILL BATTLE

ROYAL Rumble

When a king throws a party, you know it's going to be extravagant. When two kings throw the same party, that's a recipe for one of the craziest nights of all time. King Henry VIII and Francis I of France were trying to bring their nations closer together, but the night ended with Henry challenging the French monarch to a wrestling match. Henry lost, stormed off home, then teamed up with the Spanish to declare war on France. Talk about a sore loser...

PRESIDENT Of Parties

Andrew Jackson was the seventh President of the USA, but number one when it came to partying. When he was inaugurated he threw a massive party in the White House. Thousands of people came to get down and the party got so wild Jackson had to sneak out of a window. The only way to get the guests to leave the White House itself was to fill the lawn with barrels of free booze. Jackson's partying ways even earned him the nickname "King Mob".

RUSSIAN Standard

When World War Two finally came to an end, people were ready to party. Russians being Russians, they cracked open the vodka and got right to drinking. In Moscow, they partied so hard they literally drank all of the vodka in the city. There was not a drop left to be had. Bravo, Moscow.

"GINDEPENDENT WOMAN" ENAMEL PIN BADGE, £7.99, oflifeandlemons

GIN GIFT SET HAMPER, £33.99, Debenhams

PROFESSIONAL 8-PIECE COCKTAIL GIFT SET, £29.99, Lakeland

The GINPORIUM

The loveliest gin-inspired gifts for friends, family – or yourself!

SET OF 2 RINA GREEN GIN GLASSES, £19.50, oliverbonas.com

GIN BY TIM BULMER 1,000-PIECE JIGSAW PUZZLE, £21.99, The Range

THE PINK GIN GIFT SET, £26.98, Amazon

GIN AND TONIC ORGANIC LIQUID SOAP 250ML, £8.95, weegreenplace.co.uk

EAST END PRINTS GIN & TONIC PRINT, £14, Dunelm

"ALL GINS BRIGHT AND BEAUTIFUL" TOTE BAG, £12.99, notonthehighstreet.com

SET OF 3 BOXED NOVELTY GIN SOCKS, £14.99, mollieandfred.com

"GIN BUNNY" WOMEN'S T-SHIRT, £8, oflifeandlemons.co.uk

RHUBARB GIN SCENTED JAR CANDLE, £19.99, wayfair.co.uk

JOE BROWNS "LET THE FUN BE GIN" CUSHION, £30, Next

GIN THE MOOD COCKTAIL RECIPE BOOK, £8.99, Amazon

NATURAL LIP BALM – GIN & TONIC, £3.60, Goats of the Gorge

SAGE GIN AND TONIC COIN PURSE, £37, luluguinness.com

ERNE BLUSH GIN & TONIC GLASSES, SET OF 4, £35.95, Debenhams

Making It PERSONAL…

Perfect for the gin lover in your life

FROM LEFT:

PERSONALISED GIN BAR METAL SIGN, £12, Dunelm

PERSONALISED GIN AND TONIC SINGLE SLATE COASTER, £9.99, Ryman

MAY CONTAIN GIN; ENGRAVED NECKLACE, £45, notonthehighstreet.com

Words: KATRINA PATRICK
ALL PRICES CORRECT AT TIME OF GOING TO PRESS

Gin O'Clock IN NORTHERN IRELAND

Words: LUCY GALLOWAY

Done the Games of Thrones tour? Good, now it's time to play the game of gin!

Muriel's Café Bar, Belfast

Don't be fooled by the "café" in the name, this place is a little piece of gin paradise houses – sharp intake of breath – over 100 gins and offers super comfy couches to enjoy them from. It puts a whole new meaning to sofa Saturdays.

12-14 Church Lane, BT1 4QN

Rita's, Belfast

Another girl after our own hearts is Rita. Stacked in her glittering shelves is a full cabinet of curiosities for gin lovers. One of the "conditions of carriage" at Rita's is that ladies let their hair down. With such an excellent selection, it'd be rude not to.

44 Franklin St, BT2 7GE

Bentley Bar, Derry

Derry's truly a city on the up with a thriving cultural scene and as a base for exploring the Wild Atlantic Way. And, after all that sightseeing, what could be better than relaxing back in a trendy pub with a top-class G&T in hand? The Bentley Bar offers exactly that – overlooking the historic walls of Derry city centre, it has its own bespoke gin bar as well as a top-rated restaurant. Truly legen-Derry!

1-7 Market St, BT48 6EF

Galgorm Resort, Ballymena

Follow the rainbow off the beaten track to the town of Ballymena in County Antrim and you will be rewarded. Not with pots of gold, but with gin – so altogether better then. The Galgorm Resort and Spa is one such reward – and there over 300 gins to choose from. Enjoy.

136 Fenaghy Rd, BT42 1EA

The Perch, Belfast

What's better than gin, we ask? The answer is: gin on a beautiful rooftop bar in the sunshine. While we can't guarantee the sunshine, we can guarantee a wide selection of gorgeous gins at The Perch. Plus, their cocktail game is pretty impressive too.

42 Franklin St, BT2 7GE

SHAKEN And Stirred

Nine of the very best cocktail recipes for every occasion!

Clover Club

A simple yet sophisticated delight, sure to please any sweet tooth

Ingredients

50ml gin
10ml lemon juice
25ml raspberry syrup or grenadine
Dash of sugar syrup
1 egg white
Raspberries and rosemary to garnish

Method

1 Add all the ingredients to a shaker and fill with ice.
2 Shake then strain into a chilled cocktail glass.
3 Garnish with speared raspberries and rosemary sprigs.

Pictures: SHUTTERSTOCK

Elegance in a glass, this classic cocktail has a long history and zesty hit

Gimlet

Ingredients
50ml gin
25ml lime
Sugar syrup to taste
A couple of basil leaves

Method
1 Add the gin, lime juice and sugar syrup to a shaker.
2 Shake for 10 seconds.
3 Strain into an ice-filled glass.
4 Garnish with the basil.

English Garden

Light, moreish and perfect for those long summer evenings

Ingredients

65ml lemonade
50ml gin
25ml elderflower liqueur
25ml lime juice
Cucumber and edible flowers to garnish

Method

1 Stir all the ingredients except the garnishes in a small tumbler over ice.
2 Garnish with sliced cucumber and edible flowers.

Greyhound

Ingredients

50ml gin
75ml grapefruit juice
Dash of Angostura bitters
Half a pinch of sea salt
Grapes, raspberries, basil leaves and a grapefruit slice

Method

1 Dry shake the salt, grapefruit juice and gin for 10 seconds.
2 Pour into a long tumbler and garnish with the fruit and basil leaves.

Multiply the ingredients of this fruity joy into a pitcher and ask round friends!

Red Snapper

Buckle up for this fiery Bloody Mary with a gin-infused twist!

Ingredients

50ml gin
1 squeeze lemon juice
1 dash of your favourite hot sauce
1 dash Worcestershire sauce
1tsp horseradish sauce
Tomato juice
A pinch of celery salt
2 grinds black pepper
Gherkin, olive, lime and celery stick

Method

1 Add the gin, lemon juice, hot sauce, Worcestershire sauce, horseradish sauce, tomato juice and celery salt to a glass and stir.
2 Add a stick of celery, slice of lime and a speared olive and gherkin then grind black pepper over the top of the glass.

White Lady

A silky introduction into the world of egg-white based cocktails

Ingredients

50ml London dry gin
25ml Cointreau
12ml lemon juice
1 egg white
Lemon peel to garnish

Method

1 Combine all the ingredients except the lemon peel in your shaker.
2 Dry shake (without ice) until blended.
3 Shake with ice until chilled.
4 Strain into a coupe glass and garnish with the lemon peel.

Follow the method carefully here – and be sure to enjoy the buzz!

Bee's Knees

Ingredients
50ml gin
30ml lemon juice
1tbsp honey

Method
1 Add the gin, lemon juice and honey to a cocktail shaker.
2 Dry shake for 10-20 seconds. This initial shake is essential to avoid having to make a honey syrup. If you shake immediately with ice you'll end up with a very sour drink and honey coated ice cubes.
3 Add ice and shake for a further 10-15 seconds to chill.
4 Strain into a coupe glass.

Negroni

There are many variations but this version really hits the spot for us!

Ingredients
25ml gin
25ml vermouth
25ml Campari liqueur
Orange peel to garnish

Method
1 Fill a glass with ice cubes.
2 Add the gin, vermouth and Campari and stir.
3 Garnish with the orange peel.

French 75

Ingredients
50ml gin
30ml lemon juice
Sugar syrup
Champagne

Method
1 Add the lemon, sugar syrup and gin to an ice-filled shaker.
2 Shake for about 15 seconds until chilled.
3 Strain into a Champagne flute.
4 Top with Champagne, stir gently and serve with an ice cube.

The sparkle of Champers adds complexity to this ginny joy!

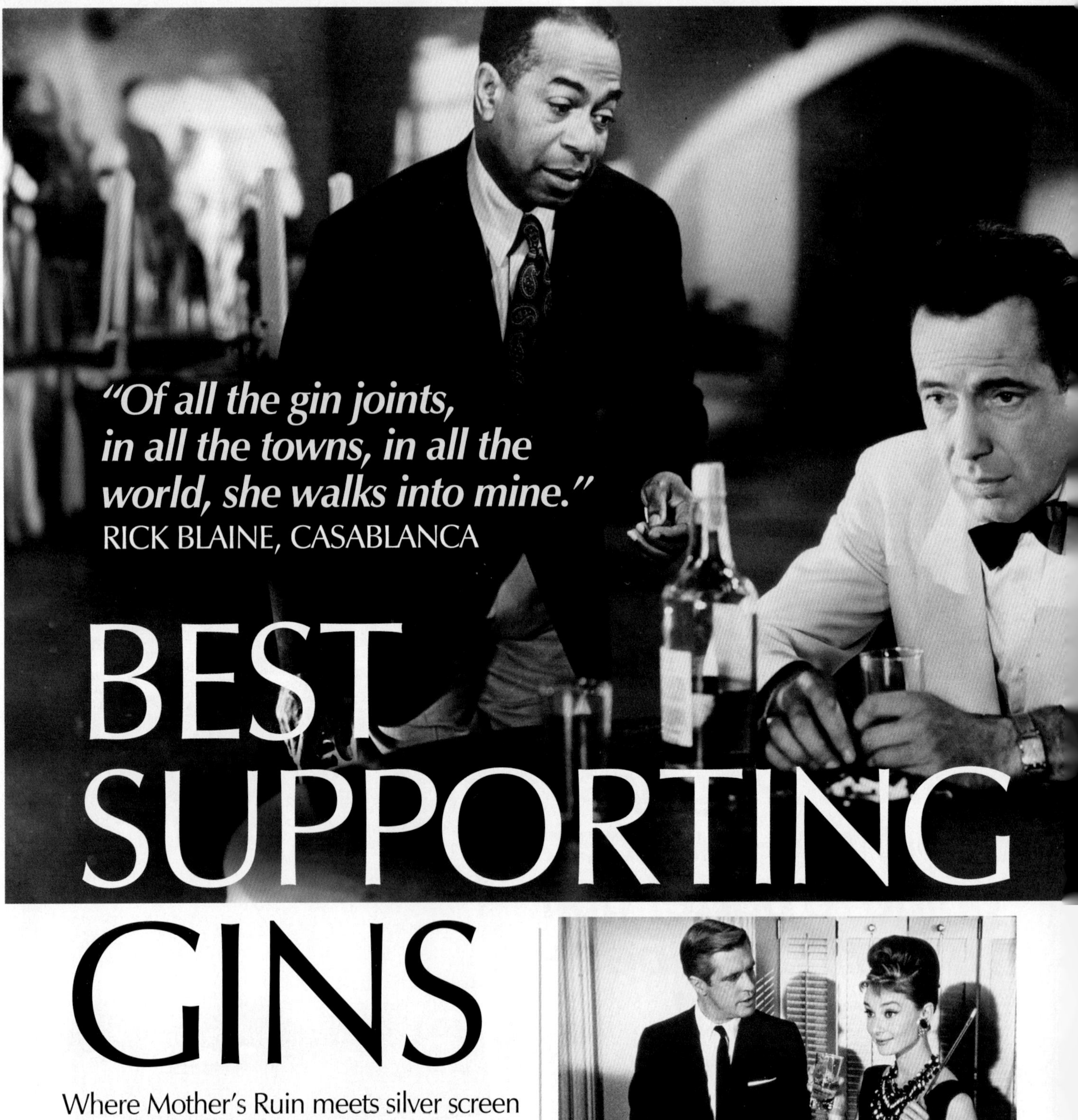

"Of all the gin joints, in all the towns, in all the world, she walks into mine."
RICK BLAINE, CASABLANCA

BEST SUPPORTING GINS

Where Mother's Ruin meets silver screen

Gin has carved a distinct place for itself in the pages of modern history. Rising from the depths of squalor where it was considered a poor man's drink, to becoming a mainstay of cocktail culture throughout the turn of the century and eventually coming into its own indie renaissance with the emergence of boutique distilleries, gin's significant impact on culture is most evident on the silver screen. Here are some the most iconic gin moments immortalised on film.

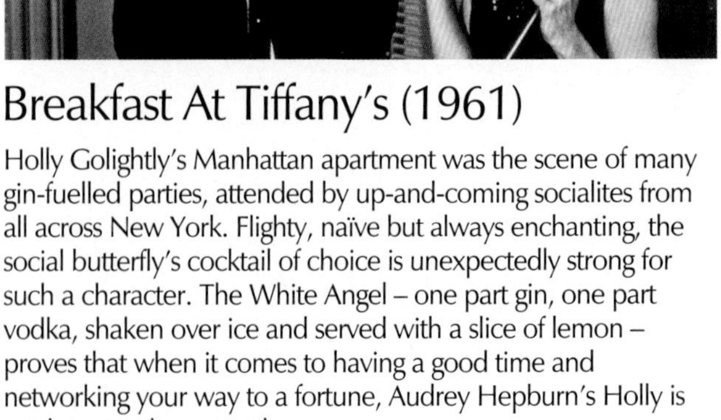

Breakfast At Tiffany's (1961)

Holly Golightly's Manhattan apartment was the scene of many gin-fuelled parties, attended by up-and-coming socialites from all across New York. Flighty, naïve but always enchanting, the social butterfly's cocktail of choice is unexpectedly strong for such a character. The White Angel – one part gin, one part vodka, shaken over ice and served with a slice of lemon – proves that when it comes to having a good time and networking your way to a fortune, Audrey Hepburn's Holly is not here to play around.

"And since gin to artifice bears the same relation as tears to mascara, her attractions at once disassembled…"

TRUMAN CAPOTE, BREAKFAST AT TIFFANY'S

Casablanca (1942)

Often regarded as the finest film to ever grace the silver screen, *Casablanca* is a tale of love, betrayal and intrigue set against the turbulent backdrop of the Second World War. Most of the action takes place in the Café Américain, the upscale nightclub owned by Humphrey Bogart's Rick. It's where he chooses to drown his heartbreak with a bottle of gin (not recommended) after encountering his long-lost lover Ilsa and her fugitive husband. His immortal words are oft referenced but no portrayal or parody sounds quite right without a glass of gin to wash it down with.

Words: LORI PETRIE

The African Queen (1951)

Africa. The outbreak of the First World War. An uptight, straight-laced Methodist missionary persuades a drunken, gin-swilling riverboat captain (Bogart, again. There may be a pattern developing here...) to attack a warship with his vessel. What could possibly go wrong? We definitely don't recommend mixing your Gordon's with the murky waters of the Congo like Captain Allnut. It might seem like a better alternative to Katharine Hepburn pouring your entire stash into the river, but trust us on this one. That's one cocktail we'd rather not try.

"Have pity, miss. I'll perish without the hair of the dog!"

CHARLIE ALLNUT, THE AFRICAN QUEEN

Casino Royale (2006)

Bond famously takes his martinis with vodka. Shaken, not stirred. Obviously. But the high-stakes poker game 007 finds himself in during *Casino Royale* calls for a drink with a little more of a kick. And so, the Vesper Martini was born. Named after the alluring double agent Vesper Lynd, the cocktail took on a life of its own after its debut in the original novel, becoming a popular choice among civilians and secret agents alike.

"My friend, make me one as well. Hold the fruit."

FELIX LEITER, CASINO ROYALE

The Great Gatsby (2013)

"Tom came back, preceding four gin rickeys that clicked full of ice. Gatsby took up his drink. 'They certainly look cool.'"

F. SCOTT FITZGERALD, THE GREAT GATSBY

Numerous gin-based concoctions were undoubtedly imbibed during the many lavish parties thrown by the titular Gatsby in Baz Luhrmann's gorgeous adaptation of the classic novel. It may come as a surprise to learn however that despite the decadence of the Roaring '20s, the drinks of the era remained on the simpler side.

In a world without air-conditioning or refrigeration, Gin Rickeys – made with gin, soda water, ice and lime – were about as fancy as you could expect. Strong enough for men to acceptably drink among polite company without hurting their masculine image but tangy and bubbly enough to appeal to the newfound liberation of the women of the decade.

Images: ALAMY, SHUTTERSTOCK

The SOBER Truth

Which hangover cures really work the morning after the gin before? We put them to the test

Words: CARA SCOTT-MORRISON

GONE are the days of stumbling home at sunrise, fresh-faced and ready to take on the world. Instead, we've reached a point where even the slightest sniff of our preferred spirit can leave us in the sorriest state. Where everything hurts – from our heads to our egos – and the loom of an existential crisis is almost as inevitable as uttering that insincere promise of "never again". Fortunately, there is hope. In a mission to vanquish the fear that accompanies waking up in a tilt-a-whirl, with a mouth drier than a bottle of London's finest, we set out to find a real "cure" for the much-dreaded hangover. Here's what we found...

CURIOUSER And CURIOUSER

The weirdest cures from around the world...

DRIED BULL PENIS
This Sicilian treatment sounds more like a cock and bull story than a delicacy.

LEMONY-FRESH ARMPIT
When life gives you lemons... stick them under your pits? Thanks for the advice, Puerto Rico.

PRAIRIE OYSTER
Oh America, why would you do this to yourself? But, in case anyone else wants to, here's the recipe...

- 1 raw egg
- 1 tsp Worcestershire sauce
- 1 dash Tabasco sauce
- Salt and pepper to season
- 25ml brandy (optional)

Pictures: SHUTTERSTOCK

1 Let's Get Physical

CURE: Exercise **THEORY:** Sweating out toxins + releasing endorphins + easing 3am kebab guilt = happy hangover
VERDICT: The mere thought of going for a run with a hangover was almost as bad as the hangover itself, so we ditched the running shoes and opted for a less strenuous, non-vomit-inducing activity. Yoga. It really helped and, if nothing else, provided a welcome distraction from our suffering.

2 Greasy Does It

CURE: The fry-up **THEORY:** Carbs + bacon = life (and something about replenishing depleted sugars)
VERDICT: Cooking was an absolute chore. Standing over a hot pan, sweating profusely, was as dreadful as it sounds, but eating? Eating was worse. After feeling two-stone heavier, the lethargy really kicked in, followed swiftly by nausea and total, unadulterated regret.

3 Pickle Your Fancy

CURE: Pickle juice **THEORY:** Salt + vinegar + electrolytes = bye bye, headache
VERDICT: Pickle fans, rejoice. Everyone else, sorry, but this seems to actually work. After a good few glugs of acidic awfulness the hangover headache did subside. Of course, we won't be trying this again any time soon. No-one likes pickles that much.

4 Hair Of The Dog

CURE: More alcohol **THEORY:** GIN + GIN = WIN
VERDICT: Stomaching the smell was the first hurdle. Keeping it down was the second. Handling the shame of cracking open a bottle at 9am was number three. Although getting merry in the morning did quickly ease our symptoms, it wasn't worth the fresh hell that rolled around at 8pm with the onset of hangover number two.